CONSCIOUS CLASSROOMS

Using Diverse Texts for Inclusion, Equity, and Justice

Cynthia,
Thank you for all your amazing work with kids & teachers!
—Ali

Allison Briceño, Ed.D., and
Claudia Rodriguez-Mojica, Ph.D.

Endorsements

"If ever there was a book for a point in time in our history, it is this one! In *Conscious Classrooms*, readers not only learn WHY the inclusion of diverse texts is critical to teaching for social justice, they also learn the HOW of selecting and teaching with these texts. A MUST read for educators in these contested times."

—Dr. Kathy Escamilla, Professor Emerita, University of Colorado, and author of *Biliteracy from the Start: Literacy Squared in Action*

"This is the book I've been waiting for in literacy teacher education! The authors expertly guide us to explore the rich diversity of children's literature while providing real examples from the classroom on how to teach across the content areas. Most importantly, they challenge us to critically analyze the texts we use with our students while they explain why representation matters. Every teacher can grow from this book, taking a step toward greater inclusion, equity, and justice in their classroom."

—Dr. Mary Amanda Stewart, author of *But Does This Work with English Learners? A Guide for English Language Arts Teachers, Grades 6–12*

"*Conscious Classrooms* not only highlights the transformational impact of diverse books, but guides us through powerful practices for maximizing their beauty. Page by page, Allison and Claudia offer a wealth of instructional supports, from a framework to guide text selection to instructional strategies for the literacy block and beyond. From read-alouds to book talks, independent reading and conferring, and of course, book clubs, they emphasize the need to create conscious spaces to engage readers, writers, social scientists (and more)!"

—Maria Nichols, literacy consultant and author of *Building Bigger Ideas: A Process for Teaching Purposeful Talk*

"Allison Briceño and Claudia Rodriguez-Mojica have joined together to craft this important work. The authors recount their own experiences as students that clearly impassion their ongoing research. From describing how schools often reflect dominant cultures and cater to their norms and comforts, to providing teachers with a way to interrupt this pattern, this book supports the authors' desire for 'EVERY child to have a positive schooling experience that supports their academic, emotional, and identity development.' Readers are challenged to 'get comfortable with the uncomfortable,' and go on a 'journey of self-reflection and growth.'"

—Dr. Adria Klein, Director of the Comprehensive Literacy Center, Saint Mary's College of California, and coauthor of *Meaningful Reading Assessment*

Table of Contents

Introduction

Why We Wrote This Book 4

Putting It into Perspective 6

Chapter 1: What Are Books That Represent Diversity? 18

Tools 30

Chapter 2: Why Use Diverse Texts? 38

Tools 50

Chapter 3: How Do I Select Diverse Books? 60

Tools 80

Chapter 4: How Do I Use Diverse Texts Across My Literacy Block? 88

Tools 110

Chapter 5: How Do I Use Diverse Texts Across the Content Areas? 118

Tools 138

Chapter 6: How Do I Navigate Tricky Student Responses? 146

Tools 166

Chapter 7: I Still Have Concerns, How Do I Move Forward? 174

Tools 190

Appendix 200

Why We Wrote This Book

Allison Briceño, Ed.D.

We, Allison and Claudia, had different schooling experiences.
As an Italian American White student, I (Allison) spoke the language of school. I saw myself in books from the beginning. I desperately wanted to grow up to be as smart as Nancy Drew (and also to have a cute boyfriend like her). I was well-behaved and therefore liked by my teachers. I was always given the benefit of the doubt—even when I did not deserve it. However, I noticed that my friends were treated differently than me based on their home background. One friend, who was definitely smarter than me but whose family was considered by the school to be "unstable," got placed in Special Education classes due to behavior issues that the school expected but never really observed. Another friend, who always got better grades than me but was from an immigrant family, had to ask me to advocate for her to be accepted into the gifted program. She ended up graduating high school in three years with a bunch of AP credits. (I didn't.) I knew I wasn't any smarter than these friends and that I didn't understand the school's sorting mechanism. However, I recognized that it worked in my favor.

I (Claudia) identify as Chicana and was identified as an "English Learner" in school. A student from a Mexican immigrant family, I was also intelligent and followed the behavioral expectations of school. However, my schooling experience was very different (more to come in Chapter 2). While I was able to conform to my school's expectations, it came at a high price. At times, I was ashamed of my parents' lack of formal education and my family's developing English. It took me years to undo the harm that was done to my sense of cultural and linguistic identity by U.S. public schools. In fact, I became a teacher educator because I wanted to support teachers, particularly bilingual teachers of color, to embrace and honor their own diverse identities so their students could do the same.

Claudia Rodriguez-Mojica, Ph.D.

Together, we believe the cost of admittance into U.S. culture is too high for students whose skin is too brown, whose tongues roll their *r*'s, who don't abide by gender norms, and the list goes painfully on. We also understand that dominant cultures are nothing new. Every country has its own version. And in every country you will find that those who do not "fit the mold" often encounter resistance and rejection. Here in the U.S., the dominant culture (although there have been some changes to this) continues to be White, able-bodied, heterosexual, male, and Christian. Schools, often a reflection of dominant cultures, therefore cater to their norms and comforts. We wrote this book to provide teachers with ways to interrupt this pattern.

We want EVERY child to have a positive schooling experience that supports their academic, emotional, and identity development. And, we know it isn't happening—yet. We are hopeful for change because we know teachers and believe in them. We are teachers. We know how important teachers are, and how undervalued they can be. We want to help teachers (re)gain the power to build on students' diverse strengths.

The following pages ask you to get comfortable with the uncomfortable, to take the status quo of your teaching and change it a bit—specifically by focusing on the literature you present to your students. Like you, we have seen books transform how a child thinks and summon their call to take up space in this world. We never cease to be amazed by how such a seemingly small move as finding characters that reflect the lives of students can be a springboard for acceptance and validation. We are so happy that you have decided to come along with us on this journey of self-reflection and growth.

Sincerely,

Allison and Claudia

Putting It into Perspective

Where We Are

The following are some important facts that ground this work. Knowing them will help you see that the need for greater inclusion is not a "nice-to-have" or just the perspective of a few. Quite the contrary, it is a fact of life in the daily existence for many children sitting in U.S. classrooms.

- 80% of U.S. teachers are White, yet over half of students nationally were students of color in 2018; 77% in California—the highest percentage among all U.S. states (California Department of Education, 2019; Geiger, 2018; National Center for Education Statistics, 2021).

- In one study, when teachers were uncomfortable with topics their elementary students raised, it showed. Young students read the teachers' physical response as discomfort and understand that certain lived experiences are not welcomed in the classroom (Jones, 2004; Picower, 2009).

- Students learn to silence their authentic narratives within school walls from a very young age and can begin to internalize messages of inferiority (Arce, 2004; Briceño et al., 2018; Brito et al., 2004; Jones, 2004).

- In public schools nationwide, students with dis/abilities are more than twice as likely to be suspended than students without dis/abilities, and Black students are three times more likely to be suspended than White students (U.S. Department of Education Office for Civil Rights, 2014).

Research shows that teachers have the largest impact on student learning (Hattie, 2012).

- Disproportionate suspension rates can be seen as early as preschool and have severe negative impacts including decreased connections with school, higher dropout rates, and higher cases of arrest and incarceration (Yang et al., 2018).

- Some teachers worry about facing parental resistance if they explore LGBTQ topics through texts (Ryan & Hermann-Wilmarth, 2018).

- In a survey, teacher candidates blamed their own education as a barrier to including diverse texts. They felt underprepared to address complex issues of race and power in their own classrooms (Riley & Crawford-Garrett, 2016).

- Research shows that teachers have the largest impact on student learning—more than any other aspect of education (Hattie, 2012).

The Power of Beliefs

Thinking about these larger, systemic issues can sometimes seem overwhelming. If the system won't change, is it hopeless? Absolutely not. *Teachers can change what they do in their classrooms.* As the last fact in the prior list suggests, you, the teacher, play a pivotal role in student outcomes. One way to respect this awesome power is to be a reflective practitioner. This means continuously examining your beliefs to see how they align with your school's culture, and how they influence the resources and instruction in your classroom.

The first step is to consider your own cultural story. You can use your background, regardless of who you are, to help you enter into this work from a place of authenticity. For instance, White teachers may need to prepare for "tricky," emotional ideas tied to their personal experiences, especially when they differ from their students. Remember, 80% of the teaching force is White, while over half of students are children of color. Add to that the United States' history of, at best, omitting non-White cultures from its teaching and texts, and the struggles we see today are inevitable. Once this is accepted as fact, White teachers can better understand that there are topics society has simply not prepared many of them to discuss. What is so encouraging is that this type of preparation is thoroughly possible. We hope this book will help you get started.

Teachers of color also have to prepare to embark on this work. For instance, overt discussions of marginalized groups may be interpreted differently for them. Black teachers who discuss a topic related to diversity might be seen as extreme or pushing an agenda. Knowing their "why" and anticipating these reactions can help them respond appropriately to these charges. Many teachers of color also have the additional task of unlearning negative feedback they absorbed in school about their own identities, languages, and cultures. This can be difficult and rightfully ignite disquieting emotions, including sorrow and resentment. Nevertheless, awareness is critical to pave the way for effective change.

The examples we listed are just a few of the ways that culture and teaching can intersect. The main point is that once you have considered your own beliefs, it is easier to choose materials that support identity formation, critical thinking, agency, and literacy development for all students. Not only will this book help you do this challenging work of reflecting on where you stand in relation to your students, but it is full of practical steps and tools to get you started. We have taken the sound pedagogical practices that help us all learn well—clear information, relevant examples, opportunities to think and apply—and woven them into every chapter.

Throughout the book, we use the term *diverse* to include the many ways people might be different from one another, such as race, ethnicity, culture, home language, immigration status, religion, sexual orientation, gender identity, dis/ability, and other aspects of identity. We use the term *dis/ability* to counteract the disrespect that *disability* has encountered in the past and to emphasize that the term is a social construct with historically arbitrary ways of defining what counts as a dis/ability (Goodley & Runswick-Cole, 2016). We like and appreciate the more popular terms, such as *culturally relevant*, *culturally responsive*, and *culturally sustaining* (among others). We use *diverse* in this text to explicitly include the wide range of student differences you are likely to encounter.

> "Once you have considered your own beliefs, it is easier to choose materials that support identity formation, critical thinking, agency, and literacy development for all students."

How This Book Helps

This book will help develop your thinking about how the books you use with your students represent them, you, and the world around you. We hope to develop readers' *critical consciousness* by (re)examining the role of power (i.e., where it comes from, who has it, what it means), how power can create (or relieve) oppression, and how to overcome pervasive myths that negatively impact students who are "different" (Freire, 1987). In addition to thinking about power, developing critical consciousness will require critical reading and listening, reinterpreting schooling, and getting comfortable with being uncomfortable (Palmer et al., 2019). Developing critical consciousness enables teachers to align their beliefs with their pedagogy to truly support *all* students (Alfaro, 2019).

Each chapter opens with a big idea that is expanded upon through research, explanations, and examples. Immediately following are tools, including templates, surveys, and lists, to help you begin to apply what you have just learned to your own classroom or school community. The chapter and the tools build on each other to facilitate success. Each chapter ends with educator "voices from the field." These educators share how they are doing this hard work in their classrooms.

Big Idea Section

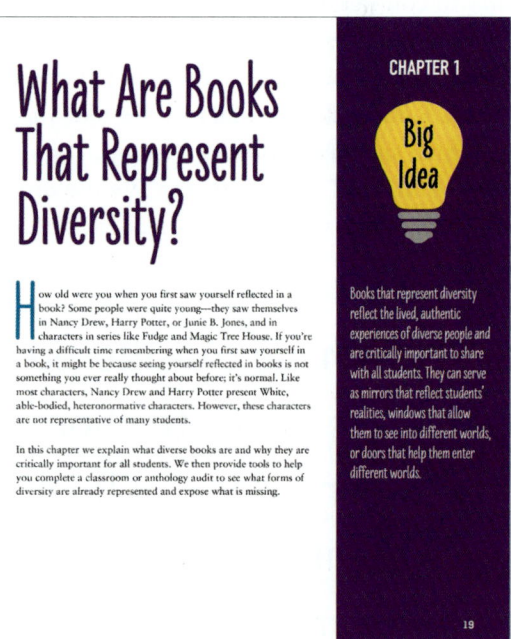

Chapter 1 begins the journey by explaining what we mean by *diversity* and which students should have access to diverse texts (preview answer: all students). It provides tools for analyzing your classroom library and curriculum. **Chapter 2** discusses why including books that represent diversity in the classroom is critical and provides tools for you to learn about your students.

Chapters 3 through 7 address the practices and beliefs of teaching with diverse texts. **Chapter 3** explains how to analyze children's books to identify which hold stereotypes and which represent authentic, lived experiences. **Chapter 4** shares classroom literacy strategies that support students' reading of diverse texts, and **Chapter 5** addresses how to use diverse texts across the curriculum. In **Chapter 6,** you'll learn some strategies to address tricky student responses during difficult conversations. Finally, **Chapter 7** invites you to consider from where your own internal resistance to using diverse books might come, and provides strategies for overcoming that personal resistance. This is hard work and we are here to support you on your journey.

Tools to Try

A New Way of Schooling

The data on schooling converges on one point: The way we are currently doing school is not working for many students of color, students who speak another language at home, students with dis/abilities, and too many others. Improving schooling for these students requires reimagining it, and then finding places where we—whatever our current role—can make change. Let's look at some examples.

Our Current System

The term *achievement gap* is commonly used to describe differences in academic performance. While the term came about to shed light on populations who were falling behind, it too often implies the students are at fault.

Deficit labels such as *English Learner, Limited English Proficient,* and *struggling readers* place the focus on what students do not know.

Schools are labeled "hard to staff" when they are in the inner city.

Schools do not value the language, culture, and skills students bring from home, and instead talk about students by their perceived deficits or dis/abilities.

Teachers require emergent bilinguals to use heavily structured sentence stems that knot up their words and impair their ability to communicate complex ideas.

Now let's consider some alternatives or ways we can reimagine schooling. Some of these ideas involve changing the terms we use or how we use them. Other ideas involve changes in our perspectives and/or our practices. Every move is significant as it contributes to a larger shift toward greater inclusion, equity, and justice for all students.

Schooling Reimagined

The term *opportunity gap* is used to focus attention on the opportunities students are given, or not, in school. It signals that teachers and students work with drastically different resources depending on location and the student population.
The term *emergent bilingual* is used to emphasize the students' bi/multilingualism. Teachers recognize that students enter school with their own language(s) and literacy practices and work to add even more.
Educators choose to work with marginalized populations because these spaces reflect their own backgrounds or because they want to rectify our country's long-standing neglect of marginalized people.
Educators recognize that students have different funds of knowledge, cultural and linguistic capital, literacy capital, and home literacy practices (Compton-Lilly & Nayan, 2016; Moll et al., 1992; Yosso, 2005).
There is flexibility in how scaffolds are offered and implemented; home language support is provided whenever possible (Rodriguez-Mojica & Briceño, 2018; Rodriguez-Mojica, 2018).

Voices from the Field

Desiree Peterson
teacher

"That message of being able to be anything I wanted to be, if I put my mind to it, was something I carried with me. This led to me never shying away from reaching my potential. I became determined to spread that same message of love and courage to children from all over the world."

Desiree Peterson is an African American kindergarten teacher at Santa Clara Unified School District in Santa Clara, California. She had been teaching for three years when we connected with her about this book. She strongly believes that students need to see positive representations of themselves starting from a very young age.

Desiree was introduced to books with African and African American characters by her dad, who made it a point to buy books where she could see herself reflected in positive and affirming ways. She said, "One example was *Amazing Grace* by Mary Hoffman. It's the story of an African American girl, Grace, who wants to perform the role of Peter Pan in her school play, but she is told by her classmates she can't be Peter Pan because she's a girl and Black." In the book, Grace's mother and grandmother tell her she can be anything she wants to be if she puts her mind to it. Grace perseveres and ends up getting the part. Desiree adds, "That message of being able to be anything I wanted to be, if I put my mind to it, was something I carried with me. This led to me never shying away from reaching my potential. I became determined to spread that same message of love and courage to children from all over the world."

Desiree works hard to create a classroom space where all her students can see positive representations of themselves. She explains, "As a double-minority, I have had several experiences where both the color of my skin and my gender influenced the way I was perceived and treated. Instead of letting those experiences keep me down, I was determined to use those experiences to empower the next generation. I wake up daily and go into my classroom with the goal of helping my students learn to appreciate where they come from and finding joy in what makes them different. I want my students to unlearn the lies that come from society that they are less than and can't reach their dreams." Desiree concluded, "In a world full of hate and darkness, opening a book and seeing someone like them succeeding is just the light they need to keep fighting for a better tomorrow."

Voices from the Field

Sarita Sundaram
teacher

An experienced, Indian American teacher in Campbell Union School District in Campbell, California, Sarita Sundaram has been using diverse texts in her classroom for many years. She explained that her interest in diverse texts started during her teacher credential program. "This is something that Dr. Andrea Whittaker taught me when I took her multicultural education course in 2004. She said that everybody is on a carousel, which leads to racist ideas. Whether you're not racist or racist, we're all heading in the same direction on the carousel. To be an anti-racist educator, you have to get off that carousel."

Sarita has been intentional about continuing her learning. She said, "This year I learned from Ibram X. Kendi's *How to be an Antiracist*, Singleton's *Courageous Conversations,* and Dr. Bettina Love's *We Want to Do More Than Survive: Abolitionist Teaching and the Pursuit of Educational Freedom*. I also attended a lot of her webinars. All of it has inspired me. I think the time is pivotal. It's really important that all educators honor the students in their classrooms by including diverse texts. It's important for students to read diverse books because it's important for Black and Brown students and LGBTQ+ students to see themselves as protagonists. It's equally important for White students to see diverse books, and see a Brown teacher or a Brown engineer or a Black doctor. Diverse texts don't help just BIPOC students; they help everybody."

Despite having grown up in India, Sarita did not see herself in books until she was an adult. She explained, "All I read was English literature. All the characters, the protagonists, were all White, White boys, White girls. Those were the only books that were available."

Sarita added, "There were comics written by Indian authors in English with protagonists who looked Indian, who had brown skin, and the settings were in India. It filled some of the gaps, but it wasn't until I was 23 or 24, when I read Arundhati Roy's book, *The God of Small Things*, that something within me shifted. The setting of the novel is the same part of India that I'm from. That was the first time I was reading something about my own culture. I could see myself as a protagonist or antagonist, and I could see characters that I could relate to. It made a big difference."

Sarita hopes that her use of diverse texts will have a similar influence on her students. She said, "Immigrants should see immigrants overcoming hurdles, Black people should see Black people overcoming hurdles. They have resilience; they solve problems. I'm hoping that this will create diverse readers and writers who own their own stories. It's not just about getting good scores and going to college. I also want them to feel like they're getting their voices heard."

Speaking about her current class of fifth graders, she said, "The students realized that they are protagonists in their own lives. And that is not just the reading, it was also the writing that opened up not just their voice, but also their sense of agency. I've definitely seen an impact this year, especially when we learned about LGBTQ+ rights. We said, 'If we are an anti-racist class, then we are not going to be making comments that are homophobic.' We talked a lot about it. And when two of my students presented on LGBTQ+ rights, one shared that her brother, who was in seventh grade, was teasing her, saying, 'I think you might be lesbian.' And she responded, 'And if I am lesbian, so what? First of all, don't use it as a slur. If I am one, it's for me to make that decision.' She had an appropriate response, and she's willing to have a conversation with her family, or anybody. Another student spoke about a time in third grade when he colored his hair and people called him 'gay.' He said, 'I wish I'd known about LGBTQ+ rights then because I would say, "You know what, it's okay to be different. I'm just exploring my identity."' I was shocked to see the levels of critical thinking that the students were able to do. The kids are amazing. The kids are ready; we have to follow their lead."

CHAPTER 1 | **What Are Books That Represent Diversity?**

What Are Books That Represent Diversity?

CHAPTER 1

How old were you when you first saw yourself reflected in a book? Some people were quite young—they saw themselves in Nancy Drew, Harry Potter, or Junie B. Jones, and in characters in series like Fudge and Magic Tree House. If you're having a difficult time remembering when you first saw yourself in a book, it might be because seeing yourself reflected in books is not something you ever really thought about before; it's normal. Like most characters, Nancy Drew and Harry Potter present White, able-bodied, heteronormative characters. However, these characters are not representative of many students.

In this chapter we explain what diverse books are and why they are critically important for all students. We then provide tools to help you complete a classroom or anthology audit to see what forms of diversity are already represented and expose what is missing.

Books that represent diversity reflect the lived, authentic experiences of diverse people and are critically important to share with all students. They can serve as mirrors that reflect students' realities, windows that allow them to see into different worlds, or doors that help them enter different worlds.

CHAPTER 1 | What Are Books That Represent Diversity?

Who Gets to Be in Books?

Students of color, multilingual students, LGBTQ+ students, students with diverse dis/abilities, and other students with "differences" have not traditionally been represented in children's books and therefore do not see themselves reflected in texts. Curricula materials also tend to omit these students and their perspectives. In fact, as of 2021, 2% of books published in the United States included Native American characters, 7% included Latinx characters, 11% included Asian/Pacific Islander characters, and 14% included African or African American characters. In contrast, over 60% of books had White characters or avoided the issue altogether by using animals or other nonhumans as characters (Cooperative Children's Book Center, 2022).

> "Students of color, multilingual students, LGBTQ+ students, students with diverse dis/abilities ... have not traditionally been represented in children's books and therefore do not see themselves reflected in texts."

If we want to include diversity in our classroom libraries, we need to be intentional about it. Thankfully, with a lot of focus and a handful of strategies, you can choose to include texts that represent your students—which makes them culturally relevant texts—in your classroom and curriculum. First, let's take some time to explain what we mean by diverse texts.

Diversity in Children's Books, 2021

The following chart indicates the percentage of U.S. published books during 2021 depicting children from diverse backgrounds or written by authors from diverse backgrounds. Note: Due to the pandemic, some publishers didn't send out review copies, so the total volume of books represented may be lower than usual.

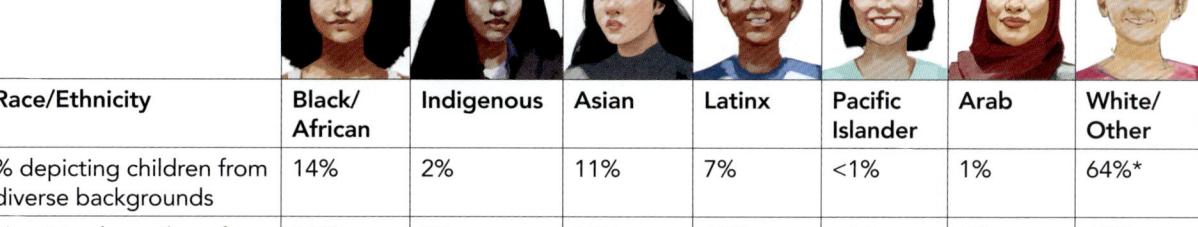

Race/Ethnicity	Black/African	Indigenous	Asian	Latinx	Pacific Islander	Arab	White/Other
% depicting children from diverse backgrounds	14%	2%	11%	7%	<1%	1%	64%*
% written by authors from diverse backgrounds	10%	1%	15%	10%	<1%	1%	62%

Data provided by the Cooperative Children's Book Center (CCBC), School of Education, University of Wisconsin-Madison. https://ccbc.education.wisc.edu/literature-resources/ccbc-diversity-statistics/books-by-about-poc-fnn/

*In 2021, CCBC did not explicitly report data for White characters/authors, nor did they distinguish the percentage of literary texts featuring animal or other nonhuman characters. The percentage shown in the White/Other column is representative of all other characters or authors combined.

Read this!

Johnson, N. J., Koss, M. D., & Martinez, M. (2018). Through the sliding glass door: #EmpowerTheReader. *The Reading Teacher, 71*(5), 569–577. This article addresses the importance of knowing our students as readers in order to connect them to books that might serve as "sliding glass doors" that open up new worlds to the students.

CHAPTER 1 | What Are Books That Represent Diversity?

Who Needs to Be in Books?

Looking at the data on the previous page makes it abundantly clear that many voices are missing from our texts. For example, Latinx Americans of the United States make up almost 20% of the population, yet are only represented in 7% of the characters and content in books. Just think of how little of that 7% actually finds its way into our classrooms. The children are there, but their stories are not.

Books that represent diversity are stories that tell the lived experiences of humans as we are and that reflect all of our human realities. They include authentic, well-developed characters that are Black, Indigenous, and other people of color (BIPOC). They include characters from non-Christian religions, multilingual characters, LGBTQ+ characters, working-class characters, and characters with dis/abilities and mental health challenges. Characters may live in different countries or be from different countries. We know that one book alone will likely not tell a student's full experience, nor does it have to. Casting the net wide increases the chances that all students have the opportunity to see more of themselves on the page.

All students benefit from seeing themselves represented in texts.

Expressions of Text Diversity

Some books represent diversity by making the "diverse" identity the central topic in the story. For example, *10,000 Dresses* written by Marcus Ewert tells the story of a transgender girl dreaming of her first dress and her parents telling her boys don't wear dresses. In *Miss Little's Gift*, author Douglas Wood tells his personal story of learning to read with ADHD. Sometimes these stories are told through animal characters instead of human characters. For example, in *Pancho Rabbit and the Coyote: A Migrant's Tale,* Duncan Tonatiuh tells a story about the hardships experienced by families separated by borders and young Pancho Rabbit's journey to help his father return home. Although the characters are not human, it is clear that the story is an immigrant tale from a Latinx person's point of view, based on its subtitle, story line, and character names.

Woodpecker Girl

Other books represent diversity by including characters with diverse identities facing the everyday struggles that all young people face. The characters' diverse identities are not the central focus in these stories. For example, *Zara's Big Messy Day (That Turned Out Okay)* written by Rebekah Borucki tells the story of seven-year-old Zara, who struggles with managing her emotions when she faces stressful situations. Like all children (and adults), Zara gets anxious at times. It is only through the illustrations that we can see that Zara is biracial and has a Black mom and a White dad. The central focus of the book is not Zara's racial identity, but learning about how to manage emotions through visualization meditation. Borucki's book features many multiracial characters without calling attention to their race in the text. This choice begins to normalize and humanize biracial characters in children's books.

CHAPTER 1 | What Are Books That Represent Diversity?

> **Quick Tip**
>
> Don't make assumptions about an author's background based on the characters or topic. If you are specifically looking for stories told from voices within that culture, do a little research.

Diverse books are especially powerful when written by authors from the communities they write about or by authors with personal knowledge about the experiences. This helps ensure that the stories are authentic and told *by* (instead of told *about*) communities. Sometimes, it is easy to learn about the diversity of the author by the pictures or information included on the back cover or inside jacket. Other times, learning more about the author will require that we dedicate a few minutes to online investigation.

> "Diverse books are especially powerful when written by authors from the communities they write about or by authors with personal knowledge about the experiences."

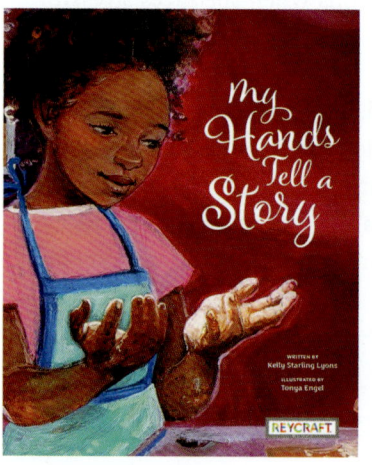

My Hands Tell a Story

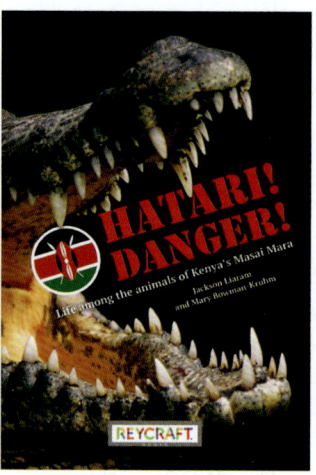

Hatari! Danger!

A Sample of Diverse Texts

We have put together a list of diverse texts in Table 1.1 to help you expand your classroom bookshelves. We selected the books because they meet the following criteria (adapted from Pennell et al., 2018):

- The characters are portrayed authentically and not pitied or patronized. The book uses respectful language. Our quick test: *Would we be embarrassed to read the book aloud in front of students from the diverse community being portrayed in the book?* If the answer was "Yes" or "Maybe," then we did not include the book in our list.

- The book is engaging and could be interesting to students from the diverse community being represented. Furthermore, students might be able to identify with the story and make meaningful connections.

- The book is easily available from booksellers.

At this stage, we are introducing diverse texts and identifying some possible characteristics. **Chapter 2** explains why we should use them with all students, and **Chapter 3** explains how to analyze and select them. **Chapters 4** and **5** show how diverse books can be used in a wide range of ways in any classroom.

CHAPTER 1 | What Are Books That Represent Diversity?

Table 1.1 Diverse Texts

	Diverse Authors/Illustrators	Black, Indigenous, and People of Color Characters	Immigrant Characters	Religious Diversity
10,000 Dresses by Marcus Ewert	X			
Miss Little's Gift by Douglas Wood	X			
Pancho Rabbit and the Coyote: A Migrant's Tale by Duncan Tonatiuh	X		X	
Zara's Big Messy Day (That Turned Out Okay) by Rebekah Borucki	X	X		
One Word from Sophia by Jim Averbeck and Yasmeen Ismail	X	X		
Antonio's Card/La tarjeta de Antonio by Rigoberto González	X	X		
Love by Matt de la Peña	X	X		X
The Powwow Thief by Joseph Bruchac	X	X		
Woodpecker Girl by Chingyen Liu and I-Tsun Chiang	X	X		
47,000 Beads by Koja Adeyoha and Angel Adeyoha	X	X		X
Moondragon in the Mosque Garden by El-Farouk Khaki and Troy Jackson	X	X		X
Ajeet Singh: The Invincible Lion by Bhajneet Singh and Guru Arjan Dev Ji	X			X
King for a Day by Rukhsana Khan	X	X		X
Yo Soy Muslim: A Father's Letter to His Daughter by Mark Gonzales	X	X		X
They Call Me Mix/Me Llaman Maestre by Lourdes Rivas	X	X		

Multilingualism	LGBTQ+ Themes	Characters from Working Class	Characters with Dis/abilities	Other Diverse Factors (e.g., Mental Health)
	X			
			X	
X		X		
				X
X	X			
		X	X	
			X	
X				
	X			
		X	X	
X			X	
X	X			

CHAPTER 1 | What Are Books That Represent Diversity?

> **Read this!**
> Iwai, Y. (2015). Using multicultural children's literature to teach diverse perspectives. *Kappa Delta Pi Record, 51*(2), 81–86. This article presents five tips for including diverse children's literature in your classroom, and includes a list of books and resources.

Benefits for Every Student

Books that represent diversity are for all children and young people. All readers deserve to experience the joy and connection found by reading stories about characters they can relate to. Furthermore, all readers deserve the opportunity to learn about the lives and experiences of people different from themselves. It is important to remember that the same book will reflect the everyday life experiences of some children and provide other children with a window into other people's lives. The opportunity to view texts through these multiple lenses creates the space for lifelong acceptance of one's self and others.

You may be asking yourself, "How will I know if the books on my classroom shelves reflect the lives of students in my class?" One way is to get to know your students and talk with them about their lives outside of school. In her book, *Cultivating Genius: An Equity Framework for Culturally and Historically Responsive Literacy* (2020), Dr. Gholdy Muhammad offers great prompts and questions you can ask students to get to know who they are as people. Here is a sample of responses completed by Isaias Aceves, a fourth-grade dual language student in Orland Unified School District in California.

> "Books that represent diversity are for all children and young people. All readers deserve to experience the joy and connection found by reading stories about characters they can relate to."

- How would you describe yourself to someone who didn't know you?

> Soy amable y responsable. Me encanta jugar con mis hermanos y amigos.

I am kind and responsible. I love to play with my siblings and friends.

- What would your other teachers say about you?

> Dirán que soy un buen estudiante. Que soy amable y cariñoso.

They would say that I am a good student. That I am kind and loving.

- What would your family say about you?

> Mi familia dice que tengo un gran corazón. Que soy bueno en fútbol.

My family says that I have a big heart. That I am good at soccer.

- How might you describe your culture and ethnicity?

> Mi cultura y etnia es alegre, llena de colores, música y baile.

My culture and ethnicity is cheerful, filled with colors, music, and dance.

- If you could take me somewhere to help me understand your culture/ethnicity, where would you take me?

> Te llevaría a México. También a una fiesta donde se puede comer comida de mi cultura como tamales y fijoles y arroz.

I would take you to Mexico. Also to a party where you could eat food from my culture, like tamales, beans, and rice.

Quick Tip

Some children may not feel comfortable talking about their lives. Don't force it! Remember, our students are not obligated to share their personal stories and when they do it is a privilege. Instead, take time to build their trust and observe how they respond to the texts that you read.

Questions from CULTIVATING GENIUS by Gholdy Muhammad. Copyright © 2020 by Gholdy Muhammad. Reprinted by permission of Scholastic Inc.

Tools to Try

Examining our classroom libraries from the perspective of diversity can be intimidating. We may have too many books, not enough books, or be unsure of what we will find. Completing an audit of your classroom library helps to identify what you really have and what books you might add to your wish list. We've provided these tools first because they can be completed before the school year begins. You do not need to complete the entire audit at once—you can spend 20 minutes after school each day for a week or two and accomplish the task. If you identify books that seem problematic, set them aside for now; we'll come back to those later in the book.

Tool 1.1 Classroom Library Audit: Overview

This tool helps you determine what topics are currently addressed by the texts in your classroom. If your school uses a published reading program for its Language Arts curriculum, you could also use this tool to audit the texts in these materials. Use a tally mark to identify the ways each text addresses diversity through either the characters or book creators. This will enable you to see an overview of the aspects of diversity currently represented in your library, and where you may have gaps.

Classroom library audits help you identify which aspects of diversity are currently represented and where you may have gaps.

Tool 1.1 Classroom Library Audit: Overview

Authentic Representation of:	Author/Illustrator	Character(s)
Asian person		
Black person		
Immigrant or refugee experience		
Indigenous person		
Latinx person		
LGBTQ+ community		
Local author or setting		
Non-Christian faith		
Person or community outside the U.S.		
Person with learning dis/ability		
Person with physical dis/ability		
Southeast Asian person		
Speaker of another language		
[insert your own criteria]		
[insert your own criteria]		
[insert your own criteria]		
[insert your own criteria]		

CHAPTER 1 | What Are Books That Represent Diversity?

> **Read this!**
>
> For additional information and another approach to auditing your classroom library, read Fishman-Weaver's (2019) article, "How to Audit Your Classroom Library for Diversity."

Tool 1.2 Classroom Library Audit: In-Depth

This tool supports an in-depth audit to give deeper understanding of what types of books you have, and which type(s) you may need. Pick up each book and look at the author, illustrator, and main characters, then carefully read the text. In the first column, write the title of the book or text and the author(s). Then, identify the various ways the book or text addresses diversity in each of the columns. For a more advanced approach, use a black pen for books that simply provide representation in each of the categories, and a different color for books that provide an abolitionist or transformative perspective.

Looking Ahead

- **Chapter 2** provides tools to help you get to know your students and consider how they might relate to different texts.
- **Chapter 3** provides tools to help you analyze and assess how well books address diversity.

Tool 1.2 Classroom Library Audit: In-Depth

Diversity Characteristics	BIPOC Characters	Characters with Dis/abilities	Characters from Working Class	Immigrant Characters	LGBTQ+ Themes	Multi-lingualism	Religious Diversity
[title/author]							
[title/author]							
[title/author]							
[title/author]							
[title/author]							
[title/author]							
[title/author]							
[title/author]							
[title/author]							

Voices from the Field

Ashley Martin
teacher

> "I had a student in my class who is African American, and I was her first Black teacher."

Ashley Martin is an experienced teacher in Mount Pleasant Elementary School District in California. A Black teacher, Ashley recalled the first time she saw herself in a book as a child. She said, "When I really think back, it was *The Doorbell Rang* by Pat Hutchins. I don't even know if they talked, but I just remember seeing them. I thought, 'Oh, there are Black characters!' At the time, I didn't think you could even color in that shade. After that, the only other time I can remember seeing Black characters in childhood was the American Girl® dolls and their books. The Black doll, Addy®, was a slave; her story was about slavery. They had different time periods, but hers was the only story that had some type of hardship; the others had their own bedrooms."

Ashley works in an urban, under-resourced school district with high percentages of Latinx students, categorized as English Learners, and students who qualify for free or reduced lunch, but very few Black students. This past school year, she explained, "I had a student in my class who is African American, and I was her first Black teacher."

She continued, "The student had issues with her hair and feeling like she didn't belong. And so I told myself, the first day of class, we're going to read *I Love My Hair!* by Natasha Anastasia Tarpley. When we read it, she was like, 'This is the book for me, I love it!' But then I thought, 'Okay, so how do I connect that book to my other students?' Other students talked about how their hair is different from a family member's, or their hair is curly versus straight or different colors. So they're able to identify, 'That's not me, but I have some similar experience.' They know I'm Black and that one student is Black. But that was the first time they had those conversations and said, 'Okay, I'm not Black, but I've also been discriminated against, or I've felt like I didn't belong.' We talked about Asian Americans, Pacific Islanders, Latinx, and African Americans."

Ashley recommended a few books that she likes to read to her students to start off the school year. She said, "My goal is to have them feel comfortable and know the classroom is a safe space. So I try to get books that represent a broad spectrum to hopefully hit everybody. *All Are Welcome* by Alexandra Penfold is a really good one. *The Day You Begin* by Jacqueline Woodson is probably my favorite. I use *Our Class Is a Family* by Shannon Olsen to set our class expectations because it shows the diversity of different people and how we can be a family even though we may not look like a family. Those are usually my top three. My goal was to expose them to people and things that they weren't used to seeing. Typically in schools we're around the same type of people. So I love books that expose students to difference. I don't want to wait for them to encounter someone and not know how to act or what to say. If you see someone that has a disability, and you've read about that disability before, you're more aware that this person is a human being. I like to expose them to as much as possible so that by the time they get into the real world, they're like, 'Oh, I've seen something like this before.'"

Ashley continued, "Last year we analyzed the books and talked about who wasn't represented in the books. I called them my changemaker group, because they were so aware of the world around them. They were really good at asking, 'Well, what about this character? Why wasn't this character put into the book?' It's joyful to be around them."

Voices from the Field

Claire Hood
teacher

"I think using picture books... is extremely effective. Because you get to have good comprehension conversations.... I would use them in middle school as well. That's what we did this year [in fifth grade]. We did a lot of picture books."

Claire Hood is an experienced White teacher in Santa Clara Unified School District in California. Having changed districts from Oakland, California, which has a larger Black population than her current school, Claire realized she needed to make some adjustments to her classroom library. She explained, "I have not had any Black students at this school. But a ton of my library is about Black history. So I thought, I need to diversify because I don't have texts that match my Latinx kids or my students from India. It's important to keep getting new books. You have to keep changing the library to update it. And also make sure that you have read the book before you read it to the class."

She explained, "I think some of the books that I really like to use are ones that reflect my students in a way that they can see themselves immediately and get that kind of connection. It's important to keep up-to-date with what's coming out, and how you can support diverse authors." When asked how she keeps up-to-date with new books, Claire mentioned the website BookRiot (https://bookriot.com/) or an Internet search for "best new diverse children's books."

Claire has taught fifth grade as well as kindergarten. She commented on the use of diverse picture books across the grades, saying, "I think using picture books, even with fifth grade, is extremely effective. Because you get to have good comprehension conversations, even though it is a picture book. I would use them in middle school as well. That's what we did this year [in fifth grade]. We did a lot of picture books."

When asked to compare what those conversations looked like in fifth grade compared to kindergarten, Claire said that fifth graders "have more background knowledge, so the conversations have more depth. In kindergarten you're often introducing a topic that they kind of know but don't have a name for. So that takes a bit more scaffolding. But with fifth grade, when you're reading a book about a student living in poverty and trying to find beauty around her, students are able to make the connections with poverty. So I think, with upper-grade kids, you get to delve a little bit deeper, but your job is still kind of the same where you want to facilitate and not run the whole conversation. If students didn't know about gay rights, for example, they get to learn it in a conversation from kids who have a little bit more background. So the kids really get to teach each other more. The conversations flow better. The students are open to everything."

CHAPTER 2 | Why Use Diverse Texts?

Why Use Diverse Texts?

CHAPTER 2

Big Idea

Positioning diversity at the center of both teaching and learning promotes greater respect and understanding among teachers and students, and helps sustain children's linguistic and cultural identities.

This chapter addresses the importance of using diverse texts in a society that views White, middle-class, English-monolingual, able-bodied, heteronormative people as "normal," and people deviating from that norm as "other" and "less than." It also explores the research base behind the concept of Culturally Sustaining Pedagogy (Paris, 2012; Paris & Alim, 2017), which is the theoretical underpinning of this book. We believe this framework is a tool to help you examine your current practices and how well they serve all of your students.

At the end of this chapter, we provide two tools to help you get to know your students and another tool to help you think about how your individual students might connect to—or not connect to—particular books.

CHAPTER 2 | Why Use Diverse Texts?

A Child's Perspective

Imagine you are a young Mexican American girl at a small rural school with a high Latinx student population. Spanish is your first language, but by fourth grade you are able to successfully engage in the school's English curriculum and instruction. While you are bilingual, you speak only Spanish at home because most of your family has not yet acquired English. Your parents immigrated to the U.S. from México before you were born, and you grew up with your extended family living at your house for different periods of time while they found work and their own home in the U.S. Your parents and extended family work as farmworkers, often from before sunrise until sunset. Your small house is often full and loud with laughter, the kitchen blender making chile and tomato sauces, and the television or radio tuned into Spanish channels. You enjoy school, for the most part, and do your homework at the kitchen table or on the bed you share with your sister. This is your home life and it feels just as normal as most home lives do.

At school, however, your home life begins to feel less normal. Most of the teachers at your school are White and few are bilingual in Spanish and English. In fourth grade, you sing "The Star-Spangled Banner" and "Take Me Out to the Ball Game" and listen to your teacher read aloud *Old Yeller* after lunch recess. During independent reading time, you reach for the Baby-Sitters Club books, *Tales of a Fourth Grade Nothing*, the Fudge series, and *Are You There God? It's Me, Margaret.* Even though most of your classmates speak Spanish and are Mexican American like you, there are no books in Spanish in the classroom library. The families in the books you read in class show a slender, light-skinned mother character greeting the children home from school with fresh-baked chocolate chip cookies. The children in the books have their own bedrooms (with fish or hamster pets!) and desks to do their homework. The families, and their dog, go on long vacations to the lake or beach. Even though no one ever explicitly tells you that "normal" families are White, speak

Lack of representation in classroom books can damage children's cultural and linguistic identities.

(only) English, and don't have family members using the living room couch as their bed at night, you slowly begin to see that your family is "different." Slowly, you share less and less about your real life in class and you begin to feel embarrassed, ashamed really, that your home life is not like those you read about in books.

If your home life were normal, wouldn't it be reflected in the books on your classroom bookshelf? Wouldn't your teacher share stories like those you lived? If being bilingual was valuable, why did it feel like your family was a nuisance when your parent-teacher conferences took longer because of the necessary translations? If being bilingual was a strength, why were there no bilingual or Spanish books in the classroom? If being a Mexican immigrant family was valued, why were you absent from the state-adopted textbooks and the books in classroom libraries?

CHAPTER 2 | Why Use Diverse Texts?

More Than Pictures and Words

Books can be windows or sliding glass doors through which students access new perspectives.

The life we just walked you through was my childhood (Claudia's). There are many adults and children today who know what it feels like to internalize negative beliefs about their family, community, traditions, and languages. Bishop (1990) explained that when children "cannot find themselves reflected in the books they read, or when the images they see are distorted, negative, or laughable, they learn a powerful lesson about how they are devalued in society" (p. ix). Children learn that books are written about important people, and important people are White, English-speaking, heterosexual, middle or upper class, Christian, and able-bodied.

So why is it important that you have diverse texts in your classroom library? Because it will communicate to all of your students that they and their families are valued. Because having diverse texts in your classroom will back you up when you tell your students that their Spanish, Vietnamese, Urdu, and Hmong are beautiful and so is their black and brown skin. It will back you up when you tell them that you believe in them all equally and will help them all succeed in your classroom.

For students who are already reflected in your classroom library, it will help them see that they are but one story and that they share space with people whose lives are just as normal as their own.

Books serve an important purpose in this development. Bishop (1990) said books can be mirrors, reflecting back a familiar story, windows that we look through to glimpse other worlds or perspectives, and sliding glass doors that we step through to enter other worlds more fully.

The lack of representation in children's literature is detrimental not only to students whose lives are outside of the "norm," but also to students who have no trouble finding themselves reflected in literature (Bishop, 1990). The lack of windows and doors into other perspectives inhibits their understanding of the diversity of the world in which they live, as well as their place in it. Considering school segregation, books may be the only places where children "meet" others unlike themselves. Bishop continues, "If they see only reflections of themselves, they will grow up with an exaggerated sense of their own importance and value in the world—a dangerous ethnocentrism." Thus, systemic racism, ableism, sexism, and heterosexism are perpetuated. Thankfully, diverse books can help us find our way out of this cycle.

> **Read this!**
>
> Bishop, R. S. (1990). Mirrors, windows, and sliding glass doors. *Perspectives*, 6(3), ix–xi. This brief, readable, seminal article explains the importance of diverse books for *all* students.

"The lack of windows and doors into other perspectives inhibits [students'] understanding of the diversity of the world in which they live, as well as their place in it."

CHAPTER 2 | Why Use Diverse Texts?

And finally, culturally relevant texts improve students' outcomes as they help students anchor comprehension to their identities and personal experiences (Gray, 2009). They also improve motivation and engagement, as students are better able to connect with the books (Alim & Paris, 2017; Christ et al., 2018). In the next section, we will explore the framework of Culturally Sustaining Pedagogy (CSP) as a vehicle for change.

Diverse texts provide role models for all children and back you up when you tell them that you believe in them all equally and will help them succeed in your classroom.

Culturally Sustaining Pedagogy (CSP)

To counter the deficit perspective about students of color that is so common in schools, Gloria Ladson-Billings researched how teachers incorporated African American students' culture into their teaching and termed it Culturally Relevant Pedagogy (CRP) (1994, 1995a, 1995b). She found that African American students had to choose between acting White to succeed in school, or showing their cultural competence among their peer group. CRP enables students to maintain their cultural integrity while succeeding academically, and it often leverages teaching strategies such as including current music in the classroom and discussing community-based issues (Ladson-Billings, 1994, 1995a, 1995b). CRP encourages reciprocal positive relationships between the teacher and students and among students to create a community of learners. It enables students to make explicit connections between school and their lived experiences.

CRP has recently evolved into CSP, or Culturally Sustaining Pedagogy (Ladson-Billings, 2014; Paris, 2012; Paris & Alim, 2017). Rather than asking teachers to only acknowledge and accept students' different backgrounds, CSP seeks to perpetuate and foster the ongoing existence of these cultures in society. The term "culturally sustaining" requires teachers to support students in the development of their identities and promote their cultural, community, and linguistic knowledge. CSP positions marginalized students at the center of teaching and learning. As a result, how teachers do school and what counts as school are questioned, including the curriculum, assessments, participation practices, rules, norms, roles of the teacher and students, and importantly, sources of power.

Quick Tip

To avoid stereotyping, remember that cultures are complex and dynamic. While many cultures have distinct features, overfocusing on any one feature can undermine true diversity. If characters from the same culture are doing the same thing in every book, you need to reevaluate your texts.

A Community Focus

CSP explicitly calls for "schooling to be a site for sustaining the cultural ways of being of communities of color" (Paris & Alim, 2017). What does this mean in practice? The key is to adapt your teaching to the local community:

- What are its strengths and challenges?

- How can the strengths be highlighted and expanded?

- What problems can students help to solve?

- What and whom do your students love and connect with?

For example, Kinloch and colleagues (2017) share how introducing writing as a form of resistance inspired their students and ultimately made them more engaged in writing. Performance arts driven by students' lived experiences can serve a similar purpose (Wong & Peña, 2017). Incorporating rap and hip-hop into the classroom can facilitate the teaching of a range of literacies and histories (Ladson-Billings, 2017), even as early as kindergarten and first grade (Meacham et al., 2019). Making explicit spaces for students to use their home language enables students to bring more of themselves into the classroom, as does including books that represent students' home cultures (Irizarry, 2017).

> "Like most humans, children want to be accepted and be seen as their whole selves."

Like most humans, children want to be accepted and be seen as their whole selves. There are repercussions when this does not happen. Many know the heavy work involved with healing negative internalized beliefs and the journey to reclaim what they, or their families, may have pushed away.

One of our favorite examples, the Native American Community Academy (NACA) in New Mexico, is an urban school that serves a wide range of primarily Native American students from diverse tribes and pueblos. Teachers integrate Native values into their courses and assess students on how they exhibit those values, as well as on traditional educational metrics. Five indigenous languages are taught at the school in accordance with the tribes' permission, using Native pedagogy such as situational Navajo teaching methods (Lee & McCarty, 2017).

Culturally Sustaining Pedagogy (CSP) supports the development of students' identities and promotes their cultural, community, and linguistic knowledge.

CHAPTER 2 | Why Use Diverse Texts?

> **Read this!**
>
> Meacham, S. J., Meacham, S., Thompson, M., & Graves, H. (2019). Hip-hop early literacy in K–1 classrooms. *The Reading Teacher*, *73*(1), 29–37. This article shares how primary teachers used hip-hop music to engage students and support their literacy development.

The Role of Diverse Texts in CSP

Although CRP and CSP have their roots in advocating for children of color, particularly Black children, their principles can apply to all historically disadvantaged people. Books are a perfect springboard for bringing the strengths and challenges of a community to the forefront. In addition to inclusion, ensuring that students are part of the curriculum provides access and makes it relevant.

Connecting books to students' lives—or making students' lives central to the curriculum—advances many educational goals. Students who connect with the material are more likely to learn from the material. Greater connections build self-esteem, which is vital to developing social-emotional intelligence. Many of the skills and concepts teachers struggle to help students learn may more easily find their way into the mind of a child who feels valued and recognized. Moreover, sustained access to such instruction nurtures the soil of cultures and ensures their ability to thrive now and in the future.

> "Connecting books to students' lives—or making students' lives central to the curriculum—advances many educational goals. Students who connect with the material are more likely to learn from the material."

Using CSP doesn't necessarily change *what* you as a teacher do on a regular basis—it changes *how* you do it. You continue to use books to create lessons that connect to content standards, scaffold for students identified as English Learners, differentiate for students with special needs, and formatively assess to determine what to teach tomorrow. However, a few important differences include:

- **The role of the teacher.** Using CSP, we develop relationships with students, identify highly engaging books based on students' cultures and interests, and scaffold students along a learning continuum. We follow students' leads, facilitate learning, and curate the classroom library based on students' backgrounds and interests.

- **The role of the student.** The student takes more of a lead in their learning in a CSP classroom. Kids teach us what they already know and share what motivates and excites them. Rather than reading only assigned texts, students have the opportunity to select from a range of texts.

- **What counts as a curriculum.** We teach based on students' strengths and lived experiences. For example, instead of using a decodable book with words like *cat*, *mat*, and *pat*, you might ask kids to develop their own poem or rap with "-at" words. Or you might use a jump rope song for shared reading instead of a Dr. Seuss book.

- **What counts as assessment and data.** We shift from looking at what students don't know to what they know and can do. Using culturally relevant texts for formative assessment enables us to better understand the skills and background knowledge students bring to school and how to help them transfer that knowledge to school settings. Shifting our assessment perspective to assets-based, and more culturally responsive assessments, enables us to see our students from a holistic perspective.

These changes will ultimately make teaching easier and more joyful for you, and they will make learning easier and more enjoyable for your students. Relationships with families will naturally shift from one-directional (teacher provides information to family), and possibly even contentious, to bidirectional and more of a team orientation, as the adults realize that they all want the same thing: what's best for the child. Considering these ideas will enable you to shift from trying to direct or mandate learning to facilitating student growth on a variety of different levels, such as identity growth, linguistic development, academic performance, social development, and emotional growth.

Tools to Try

The following tools will help you get to know your students. Remember, you should not presume to know about a child's life without taking the time to learn about it from the child, family, or caregiver. Do not let yourself fall into assumptions or stereotypes. Having one-on-one conversations with your students is the most telling and accurate way to complete these tools. After you have filled out the tools, you can compare what you learned about your students with the results from the classroom library audit tools in Chapter 1 to determine your most pressing book needs.

Tool 2.1 Getting to Know Your Students

Getting to know your students is a starting point for creating inclusive and equitable classrooms. There is a lot of self-reflection involved in answering these questions, so give students time to think through the answers. Some may not be ready or willing to answer right away. Allow them to share as much as they are comfortable with, and reflect your interest and appreciation back to them. We recommend you complete the tool for every student in your classroom at least once in the academic year.

Getting to know your students is a starting point for creating inclusive and equitable classrooms.

Tool 2.1 Getting to Know Your Students

Student Name: **Date:**

Questions	Student Response
How would you describe yourself to someone who didn't know you?	
What would your other teachers say about you?	
What would your family say about you?	
How might you describe your culture and ethnicity?	
If you could take me somewhere to help me understand your culture/ethnicity, where would you take me?	
What is special to you?	
What would you like me to know about you?	

From CULTIVATING GENIUS by Gholdy Muhammad. Copyright © 2020 by Gholdy Muhammad. Reprinted by permission of Scholastic Inc.

Tool 2.2 Caregiver Input: Getting to Know Your Child

Getting to know children's families and caregivers will help you better understand your students' lived experiences and beliefs. We use the terms *families* and *caregivers* rather than *parents* because some students live with grandparents, aunts or uncles, foster parents, or in group homes rather than with a mom and/or dad. Families and caregivers usually enjoy having an opportunity to share about their children and can provide important insights that can help you better teach your students. Reach out to them, offer to have a conversation in lieu of a written response, and withhold judgment if a caregiver does not respond.

Tool 2.2 Caregiver Input: Getting to Know Your Child

Student Name:	Date:
	Please share your responses for each row in the boxes below. Feel free to share book titles and as much information as you'd like.
Books as Mirrors Research has shown that it is important that students see their lives reflected in books. These books serve as *mirrors* into their own identities and lives. What story themes and characters would help your child see themselves reflected in books in our class?	
Books as Windows It is also important for students to learn about lives and perspectives different from their own. We call books that allow students to look into different lives *books as windows*. What story themes and characters would help your child see perspectives and lives different from their own?	
Books as Sliding Glass Doors When students really engage with a book, they can step through an imaginary door into a different world. We call books that invite students to step into a different world *books as sliding glass doors*. What themes and characters would help your child step into a world different from their own?	

Adapted from concepts developed in Bishop, R. S. (1990). Mirrors, windows, and sliding glass doors. *Perspectives*, 6(3), ix–xi.

CHAPTER 2 | Why Use Diverse Texts?

Tool 2.3 Mirrors, Windows, and Sliding Glass Doors: How Will Students Interact with This Text?

As a reminder, texts are mirrors when they reflect back students' own lives; windows when they provide a glimpse into another perspective; and, when a reader is highly engaged in a book, a sliding glass door they can step through into another world (Bishop, 1990). A book could serve as both a mirror and a window at the same time, because students, like us, are complex people with intersecting identities. The goal is to be thoughtful when planning for instruction. The insights you gain from using this tool can help you scaffold questions for comprehension and consider individual supports.

Looking Ahead

- **Chapter 3** provides tools to help you analyze and assess how well books address diversity.

- **Chapter 4** includes a lesson-planning tool and social justice–oriented prompting cards.

Tool 2.3 Mirrors, Windows, and Sliding Glass Doors: How Will Students Interact with This Text?

Text Title and Author(s):			
Student Name	Mirror (see themselves)	Window (see other perspectives)	Sliding Glass Door (step into different worlds)
Student 1			
Student 2			
Student 3			
Student 4			
Student 5			
Student 6			
Student 7			
Student 8			
Student 9			
Student 10			

Voices from the Field

Daniela Miranda
teacher

"Active listening has helped me get to know my students."

A Latinx teacher, Daniela Miranda has taught first through sixth grade and is currently a bilingual student teaching supervisor and adjunct faculty at San José State University. Daniela said, "For me, it starts with getting to know my students as human beings, helping them get to know me, building relationships and trust with them, being vulnerable with them. I've found that when there's mutual vulnerability, my students are much more open to sharing, and taking risks. I also pay attention to their conversations, and I have conversations with their families. Active listening has helped me get to know my students."

Daniela continued, "Also, I give them a reading interests survey… asking them about their interests and having them complete a learner profile. I could assume from the demographics on paper where students are coming from, but I don't want to assume their experiences. I'd rather hear it from them firsthand. I'm a storyteller when I deliver instruction. I share my story, my experience, because that's how I make sense of things. Sometimes that resonates with students. And I invite my students to share as well."

Daniela talks explicitly to her students about books being mirrors, windows, and sliding glass doors. She explained, "[They understand] that the books we'll be reading could be a mirror where we see ourselves reflected in the book, a window that allows us to peek into another's experience, or a sliding glass door where we enter the world of the storyteller."

When asked for an example, Daniela lit up and stated, "I had a sixth grader who identified as a boy with local Native roots from the Muwekma Ohlone Tribe. He wore his hair long because his family wanted him to, as one of their cultural practices. In school, he wore his hood all the time because he got a lot of slack from his peers for being a boy with long hair. Refusing to take his hood off created animosity with some teachers. It didn't bother me, so I allowed it in my class. On campus, we had another Native teacher from the Navajo Nation who wore his hair long and braided. I connected the two and they hit it off immediately. The teacher agreed to wear his hair down in solidarity with the student if he wanted him to. They conversed about tribal affiliation and customs."

She added, "I ran into my student with his family at the Stanford Powwow. His mom is a Native dancer and dance teacher. After that, he started to open up and shared that he wanted to do traditional dance. To relate to this student and others in the class, I did a read-aloud of Sherman Alexie's *The Absolutely True Diary of a Part-Time Indian*. My students were all people of color who saw themselves reflected in this book and it was a hit! Students started buying their own copies to read ahead. You could hear them talking about the book on campus, which warmed my heart and made me realize the power of what had happened. They felt seen, which lit a fire inside of them, a passion for reading that wasn't there before."

Daniela said, "Using diverse texts is so incredibly powerful. It creates an opportunity for students to be their authentic selves, to be really seen, to be vulnerable, and to be able to share their own experiences. What better way to get our students engaged in content, in books, and in being lifelong readers? If I can do that, if I can help students move forward in this global space that we share, I think we'll be much better off as a human race."

Voices from the Field

José Carlos Arriaga
teacher

"Sometimes I wonder if the conversations we have go over their heads, but when you see them applying it in real time, you realize that it's all worth it."

José Arriaga, who identifies as Latinx, is a dual language Spanish-English fourth-grade teacher at Oakland Unified School District. Like many teachers, José uses the first few weeks of school to get to know his students and build relationships. He described a gingerbread person activity that he uses: "Students fill out a gingerbread person representing all the parts of their identities. If they're immigrants, they talk about that. Afterward, they present it to their peers. That ends up being a really impactful moment because they get to learn about everyone's different walks of life. Also, kids are very honest, so they talk about their struggles as well. It helps them build community, and it provides me with valuable information that influences the way I structure my classroom."

Since José experienced his first year of teaching during the pandemic, he explored ways to get to know his students during virtual learning. He shared, "This past year, when we were teaching via Zoom, I used FLIPGRID to get them to talk about themselves in a space where they didn't feel like everybody was watching. That was really fun to experience as they got creative and presented their information like YouTube stars, influencers, and even newscasters."

FLIPGRID is an online platform where teachers and students video record themselves as parts of assignments. Student responses can be made public or private. It creates an interactive dashboard where students can respond and comment in a thread-like setting. José gave students the option to share their videos privately where only he could view them or publicly where the whole class could view them.

Once he gets to know his students, he is intentional about the texts and supplementary material integrated into his teaching. He asks himself, "Does this apply to any particular student or group of students in my classroom?" He explained, "It is not that much work to take that extra step to be inclusive or relatable to the class." José emphasized the importance of being prepared for difficult conversations. He explained, "When we're talking about a different perspective, one that students are not comfortable with, or that students have not been exposed to yet, we have to be very careful with the way we frame our questions. It is important to make sure that students' first experience with difficult conversations doesn't end on a sour note where they feel like their voices or thoughts can't be expressed in community without judgment."

José has seen the impact diverse texts can have on student interactions. He shared, "Recently, we read this book called *Those Shoes*. It was about a boy who was wearing beat-up shoes, and everybody was making fun of him. This impacted one of my students because she would wear mismatched things that were a little worn down, and the other students would point out her sense of fashion and the state of her clothes."

José engaged his class in a conversation about the text where they discussed differences in what people have and don't have, and he noticed a change following the engagement with the text. He said, "After we had that conversation, those comments whittled down and other students would comment back. They would say, 'Hey, you know, we're not supposed to say things like that.' Sometimes I wonder if the conversations we have go over their heads, but when you see them applying it in real time, you realize that it's all worth it."

CHAPTER 3 | How Do I Select Diverse Books?

How Do I Select Diverse Books?

CHAPTER 3

Big Idea

Becoming familiar with a wide range of children's books that are appropriate for the grade(s) you teach takes time, but it can be an enjoyable, informative process. It is well worth the effort because it often improves your ability to select books for different purposes and various types of readers. It also supports students' engagement and time-on-task reading, which contribute to academic achievement in literacy (Allington, 2013). When students select books they want to read, they are more likely to comprehend and read more challenging texts (Allington & McGill-Franzen, 2018).

This chapter provides criteria to help you select and use diverse texts. We consider how characters are represented and question the perspectives that are included and excluded. We also provide tools to help you think through how to successfully use texts that might be problematic (stereotypical characters, for instance). A list of useful websites for identifying diverse texts is included in the Appendix, along with questions to help you reflect on your use of diverse texts in your classroom.

Learning to select books that authentically represent diversity is a critical step. It is also important to choose diverse texts that honestly reflect where you, as the teacher, feel prepared to begin this work.

Note: Content from this chapter was previously published in *California English* (2020) under the title "Selecting and Analyzing Diverse Texts to Engage All Readers."

CHAPTER 3 | How Do I Select Diverse Books?

From Representation to Advocacy

Whether you're a seasoned social justice teacher or someone who is new to this work, there are books that will help you take the next step. We think of the books on a continuum, from those that have positive, normalizing representations of diversity to those that actively address issues of social justice and social action for underrepresented peoples.

Representation

To get started, you might choose books that simply have representation of diversity, without it playing a central role in the book. For example, in *King for a Day* (2014) by Rukhsana Khan, the main character happens to have a dis/ability. The fact that he is in a wheelchair does not impact the story, but it is present in the pictures. In fact, the book shows a character with a dis/ability successfully competing in a kite-flying contest without overtly mentioning his dis/ability.

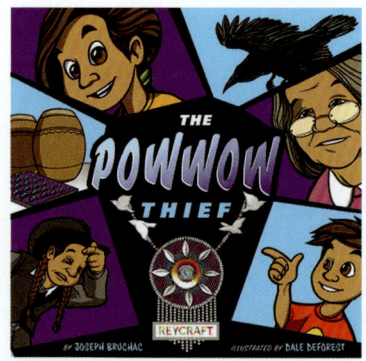

The Powwow Thief by Joseph Bruchac

A small next step in the progression might be *The Powwow Thief* (2019) by Joseph Bruchac. The main characters are Native American siblings who solve a mystery. Their race is relevant only in that they are at a powwow helping their grandparents sell Native jewelry (a piece from the collection is stolen). The setting might need explanation to students who are unfamiliar with powwows, but the book does not explicitly address social justice issues or have a call to action. Instead, it portrays the Native children as smart, competent individuals who solve a mystery. The power in this depiction is its expansion the image that Native American children can be intrepid critical thinkers and problem-solvers.

Equity Focus

Further along the continuum is the bilingual book *Mamá the Alien/Mamá la Extraterrestre* (2016), in which a child finds her immigrant mother's Resident Alien card and comes to the comical conclusion that her mother is an extraterrestrial. By the end, the mother becomes a citizen. The author, René Colato Laínez, is an immigrant from El Salvador who had his own Resident Alien card. The book introduces the topic of immigration in a child-friendly way, but does not explicitly address the debate related to immigration. The light tone allows this weighty topic to be introduced without immediately placing students in the midst of the controversy. This gives you, the teacher, more control of how in-depth you would like to go with your classroom discussion.

Progressing along the continuum, *Power Poems for Small Humans* (2019) by S. Bear Bergman is a collection of poems that reminds readers of their power when they need to be brave in the face of difficult situations. The short poems remind Black children that they carry a powerful legacy of freedom fighters, normalize diversity in families, help children navigate strong emotions, and communicate that it is noble to apologize when they do wrong. The last pages of the book encourage young readers to write their own poems that will help them remember their power. It sets the groundwork for a call to action by assuring young readers they have the strength to create change.

Advocacy

When you are ready to confront the impact of the historical exclusion of peoples and cultures from U.S. society, then Ibram X. Kendi's *Antiracist Baby* may be the text you choose. In this book, Kendi shares nine specific actions people can take to "grow to be an antiracist," including believing we will overcome racism and celebrating differences. The book provides tips for teachers or parents to begin explicit conversations about race with children. You can choose books that meet your personal comfort level and consider advancing along the continuum at your own pace. The graphic on pages 64–65 has examples of books at different places on the continuum, from representation to advocacy. Note that there is flexibility among the columns; some books could fit into different categories based on how they are used with students.

CHAPTER 3 | How Do I Select Diverse Books?

Children's Books on a Social Justice Continuum

We suggest using this table in conjunction with the social justice curriculum continuum in Chapter 5 to help you identify how different texts may fit into your curriculum.

Representation	Equity Focus
Little Thief! Chota Chor! by Vijaya Bodach recounts a Southeast Asian girl's story of a monkey who stole her toys and how she got the toys back.	*Call Me Max* by Kyle Lukoff addresses concerns of a young transgender student. Lukoff continues the story with the sequels *Max and the Talent Show* and *Max on the Farm*.
One Word from Sophia by Jim Averbeck and Yasmeen Ismail tells the story of the different ways Sophia, a Black main character, attempts to persuade her family to gift her a pet giraffe for her birthday.	*Abuelita's Secret* by Alma Flor Ada tells of a young child who, new to a school, finds his voice to talk about his Cuban culture and heritage.
Bahar, the Lucky by Rashin Kheiriyeh recounts the story of a young Iranian girl who tries to help her family out of poverty.	*The Day You Begin* by Jacqueline Woodson addresses feelings of difference. The main character is a young Black girl.
Zara's Big Messy Day (That Turned Out Okay) by Rebekah Borucki tells the story of biracial Zara who struggles with managing her emotions when she faces stressful situations.	*The Proudest Blue: A Story of Hijab and Family* by Ibtihaj Muhammad is about a young Muslim's girl reaction to her sister being bullied for wearing hijab to school.

Advocacy

Spotted Tail by David Heska Wanbli Weiden recounts the life of Spotted Tail, a Lakota chief, warrior, and diplomat. It addresses some of the complexities of Native American history and asks students to question historical practices and policies.

We Rise, We Resist, We Raise Our Voices, edited by Wade Hudson and Cheryl Willis Hudson, features poems, letters, personal essays, art, and other works by current diverse authors addressing racism and prejudice.

Stamped (for Kids): Racism, Antiracism, and You by Jason Reynolds and Ibram X. Kendi, adapted by Sonja Cherry-Paul, teaches students about where racist ideas came from and explains how to identify and stamp out racist thoughts in their own lives.

A Little Book About Activism by Courtney Ahn is a book for the youngest children, with building blocks to develop strong principles of care, empathy, and community, as well as strategies for speaking up.

Keeping Characters Real

> **Quick Tip**
>
> Note that books with stereotypes do not necessarily have to be discarded. Instead, they can be used as counterexamples that can be contrasted with more authentic books. Deep intellectual discussions and identity development can result.

Chapter 1 provided an introduction to what makes books diverse, but selecting books that authentically represent diversity can be complex. Stereotypes are everywhere—in advertisements, movies, TV shows and other media, and even in books. For example, Speedy Gonzales is the epitome of the Mexican stereotype, with his large sombrero and exaggerated Mexican Spanish accent. The mouse was so offensive that the Cartoon Network removed the character from the airwaves in 1999 (Moreno, 2016).

Even modern beloved characters are not above scrutiny. For instance, the flamboyance of Cameron from the hit television series *Modern Family* has caused some critics to question it as an authentic representation of gay life (Pugh, 2018). Stereotypes have long been used as "jokes" by comedians, the media industry, and others, but there are many negative consequences of perpetuating stereotypes, and those consequences affect our students.

> "It is critically important to distinguish between stereotypes and authentic representations in any diverse text you choose for instruction."

Differentiating between authentic and inauthentic characters can be difficult when you are unfamiliar with the lived experience of a particular group or person. Often, when people are considered different and inferior, they become the "others" or "othered" in texts, and stereotypes abound. As such, it is critically important to distinguish between stereotypes and authentic representations in any diverse text you choose for instruction. Not every example is as clear as Speedy Gonzales!

But how can a single teacher be familiar with such an infinite range of cultures and experiences? Fortunately, you do not have to be. There are a number of tools and resources savvy teachers can use to make determinations about books. Chapter 1 provided tools to help you identify representation in books and the tools in Chapter 2 helped connect those books to individual students. Now, we are deepening understanding to help you consider how to use a book with students. We will start by presenting nine key criteria to help you explore children's books and consider how to use them with students (adapted from Derman-Sparks, n.d.).

Savvy teachers can use a number of tools and resources to help them make determinations about representation in books.

Nine Criteria for Selecting Books

1. Author and illustrator. *Do the author and illustrator have the lived experiences the book seeks to represent?* If not, do they have related experiences that could qualify them to create a book about the topic? Reading about the author and illustrator can be helpful, and information about them is usually on the back cover of a paperback or the inside front flap of a hardcover book. If the answer is unclear, a quick Internet search may be helpful.

If the author and illustrator have not had the experiences the book seeks to represent, there might be a better book to address that topic of diversity. Harriet Tubman's and Frederick Douglass's books would be different if written by a White person, even if the person was an abolitionist. Their books would also be different if written by an African American Northerner who was not enslaved. This is not to say that authors and illustrators must always have the lived experience of the diversity they address in books.

Ideally, authors and illustrators should have lived the experiences about which they write.

2. Copyright date and loaded words. *Is the copyright date after 1973?* In the early 1970s, books that represented diversity began to be published. Many books that predate that era include stereotypes of women and minoritized groups, or those groups might simply be absent. While the copyright date is in no way a guarantee that a text would be appropriate or represent diversity, a good rule of thumb is to be cautious of books prior to that time.

Are there obvious loaded words that are no longer used? Is the language sexist, racist, or discriminatory in any way? Is the generic "he" used, especially for scientists, doctors, and people in power? Language changes over time, and older books may include words that are no longer appropriate in classrooms. The *Skippyjon Jones* example later in this chapter provides an example of how to use texts with more overt discriminatory overtones.

3. Illustrations. *Do the illustrations represent stereotypes?* While it may not seem like illustrations would show stereotypes, we have seen quite a few in children's books. For example, in *Chato's Kitchen*, the main character is a cat named Chato. He and his friend are wearing clothes typically associated with *cholos* or members of a Mexican American street gang: they are in red (a common gang color), wearing a flannel shirt with only the top button secured. One character wears a hat tilted sideways, and the other has a red bandana wrapped around his head. The illustrations present the cats as stereotypical cholos.

Is diversity used as tokenism? Tokenism occurs when a character that represents diversity is added arbitrarily with no ties to the plot or content. Their perspective is often not addressed, or it may be that of the White characters; they may say or do little, or simply may be silenced. Many older movies contain one person of color, often African American, who appears briefly as a bartender or waiter; their presence may be noted by the audience, but it can also be ignored as it is unrelated to the plot.

> **Quick Tip**
> Nothing can replace careful consideration of a text's content, but identifying the author's background can help.

CHAPTER 3 | How Do I Select Diverse Books?

If you are struggling to grasp how tokenism is visible in illustrations and images, consider promotional material used to market school and university programs. It is very common to see websites and announcements with people in different shades, sizes, and abilities, and the message communicated is that they represent the program itself. However, such representation is seldom the case, and people invited to be photographed often make up a very small percentage of the actual student body. They are tokenized because they give the appearance of inclusivity without the organization actually doing the work to ensure all individuals are included in practice. We make a similar argument with children's illustrations. The lone "diverse" character is often included as an afterthought to give the impression of inclusivity, but the character does not play a real role in the story.

4. Story line. The story line of a book should be respectful to all. In general, diverse texts are told from the perspective of a marginalized community. (A dominant perspective is not a diverse perspective, by definition.) As you're evaluating a book, you can ask yourself the following questions:

- *From whose perspective is the story line conceived and told?* Whose story is silenced? Is the story told from the dominant culture, or is another perspective represented? If the main characters represent diversity, are they operating entirely within dominant-culture standards? For example, is the African American character successful only in sports or music?

- *How are problems and successes defined?* Are characters that represent diversity part of the problem or the solution? Is the problem encountered by a diverse character but solved by a White male?

- *Are people who represent diversity "active" doers?* Does the character in the wheelchair simply tag along with the others? Does the character have agency? Is the female character a princess waiting to be saved by a male, or does she solve problems on her own? The question at stake here is whether the characters who represent diversity are agentive or passive? Do they encourage passivity or action, and by whom?

5. **Lifestyles.** *Are diverse characters represented as stereotypes?* Is the Chinese American mother a "Tiger Mom"? Is the gay character overly flamboyant? Are characters living in poverty portrayed as being raised by neglectful or abusive families? Or families battling addiction? These incomplete and reductive portrayals fuel future discrimination when they are planted, uncontested, into the minds of our youngest students. Instead, we want to do the work to make sure genuine lifestyles are offered and that lifestyles we may not yet fully understand are portrayed with respect and validation.

> "Incomplete and reductive portrayals fuel future discrimination when they are planted, uncontested, into the minds of our youngest students."

6. Characters and the relationships among them. *Are the characters human?* Many children's books use animals for main characters, and some do an excellent job of addressing difference and diversity. However, they are not a substitute for using books that represent human diversity in the classroom. Young children can be extremely concrete thinkers and some need multiple access points for these important discussions.

Who holds the power? Who has agency? Consider which characters hold power, make decisions, and influence others; which characters act at the behest of others; and which characters are silenced. Are only traditional gender and family roles represented? Power and agency are often implied rather than explicit in fiction, so you may have to actively look for them.

Who are the heroes, and whose interests do they serve? Are the heroes White and the villains people of color? Are the heroes stabilizing the status quo or pushing at the boundaries of inclusion? Are nuances missing in an oversimplification of a complex story?

Consider which characters hold power, make decisions, and influence others to help you determine the authenticity of diverse representation in a text.

7. **Author's perspective.** *From what perspective is the author writing?* Authors are human and therefore not objective; they write from cultural and personal perspectives. Is it a Eurocentric perspective? Middle-class? Patriarchal? None of those perspectives are good or bad in themselves, but since they represent the status quo, they are more difficult to identify. The ability to identify an author's perspective enables a teacher to address it. Consider whose perspective is presented and whose is silenced; ensure you have a wide array of authors represented.

8. **Historical and cultural perspectives.** *Whose historical or cultural perspective is told or valued? Is it still all about Paul Bunyan and Athena?* Happily, in recent years more perspectives are being included. But you must still deliberately look for texts that represent other perspectives and cultures, particularly when using historical fiction. Note that myths, legends, folktales, and fairy tales represent how people used to live and are designed to teach important cultural lessons. However, it is also important to teach about how people live in the current day and to distinguish between the historical context and now.

9. **Effects on a child's self-image.** *Are there characters with whom children can positively self-identify?* Or are there negative stereotypes that could reinforce what children see in the media? Since books traditionally have represented White, able-bodied, Christian children, incorporating books with diverse characters provides opportunities for students to encounter mirrors, windows, and sliding glass doors into different lifestyles and cultures, as discussed in Chapter 2.

> **Read this!**
>
> Schwartz, K. (2016, June 20). 20 books featuring diverse characters to inspire connection and empathy. *KQED.* https://www.kqed.org/mindshift/45121/20-books-featuring-diverse-characters-to-inspire-connection-and-empathy. This blog lists 20 diverse children's books for elementary through middle school children. It includes a brief plot summary of each book.

Analysis in Action

Tools 3.1 and 3.2 can help teachers think through some of these criteria. The tools are based on Derman-Sparks's (n.d.) "Ten quick ways to analyze children's books for sexism and racism." Just because we loved a book as a child does not mean it is appropriate for today's schools. With practice, analyzing books for diversity and representation will become second nature.

On pages 75–77, there is a completed organizer for Tool 3.1, Analyzing Texts for Diversity and Representation. The nine criteria are applied to *Skippyjon Jones* (2005) to show the challenges and opportunities of using the book with students. First, the possible issues or challenges in the text were identified. Then, ways to address those challenges were considered. Tool 3.1 represents the process of thinking through how to use the text with students. During class discussions, model your thinking so that children can slowly take on similar thinking, developing criticality about texts. For an in-depth analysis of *Skippyjon Jones*, see Martínez-Roldán (2013).

> "Just because we loved a book as a child does not mean it is appropriate for today's schools. With practice, analyzing books for diversity and representation will become second nature."

Tool 3.1 Analyzing a Text for Diversity and Representation

Text Title: *Skippyjon Jones* (2005) by Judy Schachner

Evaluation Criteria	Possible Issues with the Text	Ways to Address Issues
1. Backgrounds of author and illustrator? - Author and illustrator: Judy Schachner - Background: According to her website, Judy grew up Irish Catholic in a working-class family. In an interview, she shared that she always wanted to speak different languages.	Rather than promote and value bilingualism, the Spanish in the book makes fun of the Spanish language and its speakers. The setting of the book is "old Mexico." The language and setting are not a respectful or authentic representation of the Spanish language or of Mexico.	Problematize the use of the Spanish language and representation of Mexico. How does the author make fun of Spanish speakers in the book? How similar is the Mexico in the book to the Mexico students know? Highlight and discuss bilingualism and Mexico, and find ways to elevate the Spanish language.
2. Copyright date (post-1973) and loaded words? - Published in 2005	The Chihuahuas that live in old Mexico are described as going "crazy loco" and as having a "fiesta" and "siesta." These words all have negative connotations, portraying the characters as wild and lazy.	Invite students to brainstorm words that would describe the Chihuahuas as smart, hardworking characters.
3. Illustrations? - Stereotypes - Tokenism	The illustrations show the Chihuahuas as wild and unintelligent.	Invite students to draw alternative illustrations that undo the stereotypes and are respectful representations.
4. Story line? - Perspective - Problems and success	Skippyjon Jones, a Siamese cat from America, thinks he is a Chihuahua that speaks "Spanish." He travels to old Mexico and meets a band of Chihuahuas. Skippy (now Skippito) helps the band of Chihuahuas fight off a bumblebee bandit. The Mexican Chihuahuas are represented as needing help from Skippy, who is from the U.S., showing an unequal power dynamic.	Invite students to rewrite this story from a different perspective or with a problem or success that is a counternarrative to the stereotypes portrayed in the book.

CHAPTER 3 | How Do I Select Diverse Books?

Evaluation Criteria	Possible Issues with the Text	Ways to Address Issues
5. Lifestyles represented? - Stereotypes - Comparison with White middle class as the "standard"	Skippyjon Jones speaks with an exaggerated Spanish accent ("My ears are too beeg for my head. My head ees too beeg for my body …"), uses stereotypical Spanish terms like "¡Ay, caramba!," and adds the "-ito" diminutive to words to make them "Spanish" (Skippito). This representation mocks the Spanish language and its speakers.	Invite students to draw alternative illustrations and write text that could make this story respectful. Have students compare and contrast this book with other texts' representations of Mexican or Mexican American characters, such as *Dreamers* by Yuyi Morales or *Carmela Full of Wishes* by Matt de la Peña.
6. Relationships among characters? - Human or animal - Power and agency - Heroes, villains, and interests served	All characters are animals. Skippy, the American Siamese cat, is the hero, the band of Chihuahuas are the victims, and Alfredo Buzzito, the bumblebee, is the villain.	Using animals for characters enables the text to be presented as funny. Have students consider how the text would feel if the characters were human—particularly Mexican or Mexican American.
7. Author's perspective? - What perspectives are present? Absent?	The author's perspective as an American White woman who does not speak Spanish is seen throughout the text. The author's acknowledgment at the beginning of the book communicates that Hispanic adolescents helped give her Spanish lessons for El Skippito's Spanish.	Ask students to consider how the book might be different if a Mexican or Mexican American author wrote it. You might also consider the role of the adolescents who helped the author and ask your students if they think the adolescents would want their culture to be portrayed that way.
8. Historical and cultural perspectives? - Historical and/or cultural perspectives valued? Absent?	There are no historical or cultural perspectives present. The reference to beans, rice, siestas, and fiestas does not provide a Mexican cultural perspective; it provides a stereotypical perspective.	Ask students to consider what the book would be like without cultural misrepresentations. Would it still be "funny"? Why or why not?

Evaluation Criteria	Possible Issues with the Text	Ways to Address Issues
9. Effects on a child's self-image? - Stereotypes - Opportunities for identification with underrepresented characters	The most notably harmful stereotype is how the text makes fun of the Spanish language and its speakers. The use of Mock Spanish and the resulting laughter it causes when read aloud could humiliate students learning English to the point that they choose to speak less or do not want their Spanish-speaking family around their classroom.	Ask students to consider why the Spanish words are supposed to be funny. Who is laughing at what? Be specific to identify that a people's culture and language are being mocked, unkindly.

Adapted from Derman-Sparks, L., & A.B.C. Task Force. (n.d.). Ten quick ways to analyze children's books for sexism and racism. https://www.teachingforchange.org/wp-content/uploads/2012/08/ec_tenquickways_english.pdf

Taking a closer look at the book *Skippyjon Jones* using Tool 3.1, we can see that the text has several shortcomings that teachers using the book should be aware of. For example, likely in an attempt to be comical, the text mocks the Spanish language and its speakers with an exaggerated Spanish accent ("My ears are too beeg for my head. My head ees too beeg for my body …"). While some teachers may enjoy reading the book aloud and appreciate their students' engagement as they laugh out loud, the mocking could negatively impact how Spanish-speaking children see themselves and their families. The use of Mock Spanish could also negatively impact how non-Spanish-speaking children view Spanish speakers and their speech. It is helpful for teachers to be aware of a text's diversity and representation issues so that, if they choose to use it, they can address the issues. The third column of Tool 3.1 offers suggestions of how teachers may address issues in a text. In the case of *Skippyjon Jones*, we invite teachers to ask their students why the Spanish words are supposed to be funny and consider who is laughing at what and whom. By analyzing texts for diversity and representation, teachers can be better prepared to address issues in texts when they use them in class.

> **Read this!**
>
> Thomas, E. E. (2016). Stories still matter: Rethinking the role of diverse children's literature today. *Language Arts, 94*(2), 112–119. This article addresses the importance of diverse literature and explores the stereotypes that are often still present. It asks teachers to *decolonize* the literature used in their classrooms.

CHAPTER 3 | How Do I Select Diverse Books?

Identifying and Acquiring Books

Texts that represent diversity can be found in numerous genres and places. Although many curriculum companies are getting better at including diverse literature in their programs, teachers often want more options and look to supplement from elsewhere. Where can books that represent diversity be found? All you need to do is ask! Common sources for books include: (1) online resources, (2) families, friends, and colleagues, (3) local organizations, (4) museum and other specialty websites, and (5) garage and library sales.

- There are many **online resources** and **book lists** available to support teachers' use of texts that represent diversity in the classroom. A list of helpful websites is provided in the Appendix on page 200. Two of our favorites are Learning for Justice (formerly Teaching Tolerance, https://www.learningforjustice.org/) and Social Justice Books (https://socialjusticebooks.org/).

- **Family, friends, colleagues, librarians, students,** and **students' families** are all wonderful resources to tap for book and resource suggestions. Students' families are generally the most enthusiastic and underused resources. Since we often want to reflect students' cultures and experiences in our classrooms, who better to ask for books, stories, and legends than the students' families? Oral histories are texts, so caregivers can also participate by orally telling a story.

  With the caregiver's permission and participation, you may choose to transcribe an oral history and create a book that could be illustrated by the students. Close collaboration with the caregiver would be important for accurate representation.

- There are often **local or national advocacy organizations** that can offer suggestions for texts that represent diversity and cultural expertise. Local churches or community groups can also be good sources of cultural expertise.

- **Museums** and **other specialty organizations** often offer a lot of content on their websites. These can provide background information to you and your students as you participate in a collaborative journey to explore different people and cultures.

- Free or low-cost books are often available at **garage sales** and **library sales**. Often, simply identifying yourself as a teacher will result in a significant discount in these settings. (Bring your school ID!) Now that you have the tools to select books that represent diversity, you can easily sift through a box of books at a garage or library sale!

There are many online resources and book lists available to support teachers' use of texts that represent diversity in the classroom.

Tools to Try

Tools 3.1 and 3.2 serve similar purposes—they are intended to help you think through possible concerns with diverse texts and how you might handle those concerns when teaching. Taking a few minutes to analyze books before you use them in class helps you identify potential troublesome spots and think through how you might address them before the students are in front of you. These tools will quickly become second nature—or a consistent way of thinking—and you may use a less formal approach.

Tool 3.1 Analyzing a Text for Diversity and Representation

If you are new to this thinking, this tool helps you analyze one book at a time, prompting you with detailed questions to answer about many aspects of the book. The multifactorial analysis will help you get a comprehensive sense of how well a book represents diversity and where it falls short. The tool also provides a column for you to brainstorm how to deal with potentially problematic aspects of the text.

Publishers and curriculum companies are getting better at including diverse literature.

Tool 3.1 Analyzing a Text for Diversity and Representation

Evaluation Criteria	Possible Issues with the Text	Ways to Address Issues
1. Backgrounds of author and illustrator?		
2. Copyright date (post-1973) and loaded words?		
3. Illustrations? - Stereotypes - Tokenism		
4. Story line? - Perspective - Problems and success		
5. Lifestyles represented? - Stereotypes - Comparison with White middle class as the "standard"		
6. Relationships among characters? - Human or animal - Power and agency - Heroes, villains, and interests served		
7. Author's perspective? - What perspectives are present? Absent?		
8. Historical and cultural perspectives? - Historical and/or cultural perspectives valued? Absent?		
9. Effects on a child's self-image? - Stereotypes - Opportunities for identification with underrepresented characters		

Adapted from Derman-Sparks, L., & A.B.C. Task Force. (n.d.). Ten quick ways to analyze children's books for sexism and racism. https://www.teachingforchange.org/wp-content/uploads/2012/08/ec_tenquickways_english.pdf

CHAPTER 3 | How Do I Select Diverse Books?

Tool 3.2 Analyzing Across Multiple Texts for Diversity and Representation

This tool is intended for more experienced teachers to look across different texts they plan to use in a unit to ensure that multiple perspectives are being addressed. It poses the same questions as Tool 3.1, but it is designed to help more practiced teachers who are ready to consider various texts across the curriculum or within a particular unit. Using this tool helps you efficiently zoom out to ensure representation and diversity are strong in all of the curriculum texts, not just one or two books that will check a box.

Looking Ahead

- **Chapter 4** includes a lesson-planning tool and social justice–oriented prompting cards.
- **Chapter 5** provides tools to help you incorporate diverse texts across the curriculum.

Tool 3.2 Analyzing Across Multiple Texts for Diversity and Representation

Evaluation Criteria	Title:	Title:	Title:
1. Backgrounds of author and illustrator?			
2. Copyright date (post-1973) and loaded words?			
3. Illustrations? - Stereotypes - Tokenism			
4. Story line? - Perspective - Problems and success			
5. Lifestyles represented? - Stereotypes - Comparison with White middle class as the "standard"			
6. Relationships among characters? - Human or animal - Power and agency - Heroes, villains, and interests served			
7. Author's perspective? - What perspectives are present? Absent?			
8. Historical and cultural perspectives? - Historical and/or cultural perspectives valued? Absent?			
9. Effects on a child's self-image? - Stereotypes - Opportunities for identification with underrepresented characters			

Adapted from Derman-Sparks, L., & A.B.C. Task Force. (n.d.). Ten quick ways to analyze children's books for sexism and racism. https://www.teachingforchange.org/wp-content/uploads/2012/08/ec_tenquickways_english.pdf

Voices from the Field

Casey Cissna
instructional coach

"I am constantly on a book hunt, talking to educators and librarians across the district to learn about new, quality releases."

Casey, a White instructional coach at Mountain View Whisman School District in Mountain View, California, has been working to diversify her children's literature collection for some time. She has sought book recommendations from teacher education faculty, teachers, and librarians. Casey shares, "I am constantly on a book hunt, talking to educators and librarians across the district to learn about new, quality releases." She takes special care in the books she uses, however. "I take the time to sit down and review each book in depth. I analyze the book for general accuracy and consider the possible themes of the story. I also consider the author's background knowledge, and I investigate any stereotypes that may be present. I'm looking for value and respect for the culture or perspective being shared. Because multicultural literature helps students construct their view of the world, and of themselves, so it is critical that each book is thoroughly explored before adding it to my collection!"

Although Casey works to screen books before adding them to her classroom library, she is still learning and sometimes misses stereotypes or problematic story lines. She shared, "Sometimes a student shares a perspective I did not yet consider, and it's such an amazing opportunity to discuss with my students. We focus a lot on empathy and considering how the characters may feel. This is especially true when I find stereotypes in curriculum material, such as readings or excerpts. I work with the students to consider: 'Why did the author include this? Whose perspective is it? What are some other points of view?'"

When it comes to helping connect diverse books to learners, Casey recommends "... an extensive classroom library selection of quality literature. Each week, I choose one multicultural children's book to highlight with my third graders. Throughout the week we read, discuss, and analyze the characters of the book together as a class. Then, we vote on the theme and place an image of the book on our theme board! Over time, it is really amazing to see the theme board grow with such a wide collection of books we have reviewed!"

Cost can sometimes be a challenge for teachers looking to expand their classroom libraries. Casey has learned to be resourceful in securing the funds needed to have diverse books for her students. She explains, "I fundraised to purchase the books through various online platforms. I also applied for local grants and received donated new books from bookstores in the area. We have so many people in our communities who are passionate about diversifying perspectives in children's literature, and I found that collaborating with others really made an impact in the process!"

Casey encourages teachers to "consider many voices, and don't be afraid to empower those voices. Read books that other educators may shy away from. Have those conversations with your kids. At the end of the day, it's about diversifying the understanding that each child has of the world. Your students have an immense capacity to empathize, analyze, and construct meaning—let them explore the world around them through quality multicultural literature."

Voices from the Field

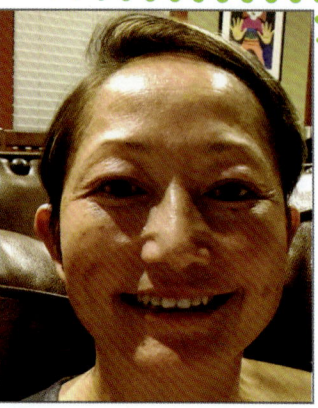

Nong Vang
teacher

"You have to raise students' level of consciousness—it's not just teaching the three Rs."

A Hmong American pre-service teacher interested in anti-racist education, Nong Vang is already using diverse books and considering how to positively influence her school community. She and her pre-service cohort have created a shared list of diverse children's books that they vet to make it easier to find books on certain topics. She said, "I've also gone on the Internet and scoured. I do a lot of research to make sure it's appropriate."

Nong likes to connect the books she uses to the students in her class, saying, "I study the students, the demographic makeup, whether it's socioeconomic, ethnic, or sexual orientation, or through getting to know their families. And then I choose books that I think would represent those students. We expand as the year moves on… to perhaps include people who fall outside of the current demographics of the class, to give [students] exposure to other things. But I think that it's really important initially to have them see themselves in literature first, and then move on from there. That initial connection will allow them to then connect to books that don't necessarily represent them. And it's easier for them to relate to if they have classmates who are of that particular background [of a book]. Then everybody can have a voice. It makes it more real."

Nong also explained how she teaches students to read books that do not include diversity, stating, "One of the ways I teach them to read is through the lens of socioeconomics. For example, 'There were people in the book who were socioeconomically disadvantaged. How can you tell?' There was also an elderly lady in the book who was very lonely. I said, 'Well, what do you think happens when people get old and their partner dies? How do you think that would feel?' I try to attach it to universal themes that many people can relate to. If you are ever given a book that isn't representative of some of the student population, you can still find universal themes in there that everybody can relate to."

Noticing that diverse literature was not common in the school where she did her student teaching, she said, "It was very clear that the teachers had not looked into diverse books. They were given a directive that this year they're going to be focusing on diversity. And I guess I shouldn't have been surprised. The reality of what's missing out there hit me. I was given the opportunity to record read-alouds and I decided to choose books that represented my first graders. I had looked through the curriculum—it's all animals and White people. So I chose books that represented the students in my class, like *Ganesha's Sweet Tooth*, which is about a Hindu god and his love of sweets. I read *Julián Is a Mermaid*. I read a couple of books on Asian Americans and Latinx people. Many teachers don't even try to do that, because it's not their reality. All this social justice stuff that we talk about doesn't exist for them. It doesn't have to. When you're privileged, it doesn't have to. I have my own privileges. I understand that."

Explaining what drives her to do this work, Nong said, "You have to raise students' level of consciousness—it's not just teaching the three Rs. We have a majority of teachers out there who are White, and some don't even see that it's relevant. They don't even recognize students' funds of knowledge. How do you change the system when the system is so entrenched in keeping itself going the way it is, the status quo? If we want to make changes, we have to work really hard to do that."

CHAPTER 4 | How Do I Use Diverse Texts Across My Literacy Block?

CHAPTER 4

How Do I Use Diverse Texts Across My Literacy Block?

Big Idea

We can—and should—use diverse texts all the time during our regular literacy practices. Integrating them into our everyday activities is simple!

You can use diverse texts throughout your regular literacy practices, not only on special occasions or during particular months. Furthermore, your literacy practices, such as interactive read-alouds, small-group reading, book clubs, and book talks, do not have to change significantly. There are ways to make the integration of diverse texts and other curricular goals seamless.

The Common Core State Standards (CCSS) identify skills that students should be able to do by the end of a grade or grade band; they do not stipulate how those goals should be achieved or the materials used on the journey. In fact, they explicitly state, "Teachers are thus free to provide students with whatever tools and knowledge their professional judgment and experience identify as most helpful for meeting the goals set out in the Standards" (Introduction to the English Language Arts Common Core State Standards, 2010). Therefore, teachers can select materials that best address their students' identities, learning needs, and styles.

In this chapter, we share strategies for using diverse texts to meet standards; we focus on the CCSS in English Language Arts. We hope you find the sample lesson plan template useful to align diverse texts with standards while developing students' criticality. Criticality focuses on the ways that classroom instruction engages students' thinking about equity and disrupts unjust treatment (Muhammad, 2020).

CHAPTER 4 | How Do I Use Diverse Texts Across My Literacy Block?

A Little Proof

Reading standards, as well as other standards, can be met using diverse books. As an example, we list the kindergarten and Grade 4 CCSS Reading Literature standards below and show that each one can be addressed through diverse books.

Kindergarten Reading Literature Common Core State Standards	Can it be addressed through diverse books? (Yes/No)
K.1 With prompting and support, ask and answer questions about key details in a text.	Yes
K.2 With prompting and support, retell familiar stories, including key details.	Yes
K.3 With prompting and support, identify characters, settings, and major events in a story.	Yes
K.4 Ask and answer questions about unknown words in a text.	Yes
K.5 Recognize common types of texts (e.g., storybooks, poems).	Yes
K.6 With prompting and support, name the author and illustrator of a story and define the role of each in telling the story.	Yes
K.7 With prompting and support, describe the relationship between illustrations and the story in which they appear (e.g., what moment in a story an illustration depicts).	Yes
K.8 Not applicable to literature.	n/a
K.9 With prompting and support, compare and contrast the adventures and experiences of characters in familiar stories.	Yes
K.10 Actively engage in group reading activities with purpose and understanding.	Yes

Grade 4 Reading Literature Common Core State Standards	Can it be addressed through diverse books? (Yes/No)
4.1 Refer to details and examples in a text when explaining what the text says explicitly and when drawing inferences from the text.	Yes
4.2 Determine a theme of a story, drama, or poem from details in the text; summarize the text.	Yes
4.3 Describe in depth a character, setting, or event in a story or drama, drawing on specific details in the text (e.g., a character's thoughts, words, or actions).	Yes
4.4 Determine the meaning of words and phrases as they are used in a text, including those that allude to significant characters found in mythology (e.g., Herculean).	Yes
4.5 Explain major differences between poems, drama, and prose, and refer to the structural elements of poems (e.g., verse, rhythm, meter) and drama (e.g., casts of characters, settings, descriptions, dialogue, stage directions) when writing or speaking about a text.	Yes
4.6 Compare and contrast the point of view from which different stories are narrated, including the difference between first- and third-person narrations.	Yes
4.7 Make connections between the text of a story or drama and a visual or oral presentation of the text, identifying where each version reflects specific descriptions and directions in the text.	Yes
4.8 Not applicable to literature.	n/a
4.9 Compare and contrast the treatment of similar themes and topics (e.g., opposition of good and evil) and patterns of events (e.g., the quest) in stories, myths, and traditional literature from different cultures.	Yes
4.10 By the end of the year, read and comprehend literature, including stories, dramas, and poetry, in the Grades 4–5 text complexity band proficiently, with scaffolding as needed at the high end of the range.	Yes

CHAPTER 4 | How Do I Use Diverse Texts Across My Literacy Block?

Diverse texts may be used to meet standards and achieve learning objectives across all aspects of the literacy block.

Reading and Writing for Justice

In the following sections we will share how you can use different parts of your reading block to advance diversity goals. We will show you how you can keep some frameworks that already exist in your classroom and alter them slightly to include and expose the realities of people from various walks of life. These small moves, done consistently, can make giant strides toward providing more equitable instruction for all your students.

Interactive Read-Alouds

We start here because interactive read-alouds are an easy way to introduce diverse texts into the classroom. Read-alouds are a teacher-directed activity—you choose the text and have full control of how it is presented, the objective, and the questions used for discussion. This high level of teacher control makes interactive read-alouds an easy starting point for introducing diverse texts to students.

Books used for read-alouds should be kept accessible for students to read independently. Since the students already know the story, books that have been read aloud are more accessible, even if they might be at a more complex level than a student can normally read. Spending time with the story and pictures can deepen students' understanding as they think through the complex issues diverse books present. And, having diverse read-aloud books accessible supports students to self-select these books for independent reading. On the following pages, you will find an example lesson plan.

CHAPTER 4 | How Do I Use Diverse Texts Across My Literacy Block?

Woodpecker Girl

Sample Lesson Plan: *Woodpecker Girl* by Chingyen Liu and I-Tsun Chiang

Woodpecker Girl (2020) by Chingyen Liu and I-Tsun Chiang, is a story about a real child, Yipei, who had cerebral palsy and resulting physical dis/abilities from birth. Yipei learned to paint and write using her head, overcoming her dis/ability and achieving more than people thought she could.

Lesson Title: Describing Yipei	**Grade Level: 3**
Teacher Name: Briceño	**Anticipated Time/Length:** 20–25 minutes
Student Identities: Use the results from Tool 2.1 to draft a list of your students' identities here. (*Adapted from Muhammad, 2020*)	• Bilingual (multiple languages) • Taiwanese American • Vietnamese American • Mexican American
Diverse Text Title and Author	*Woodpecker Girl* (2020) by Chingyen Liu and I-Tsun Chiang
Diverse Text Rationale: Why did you select this diverse text? What aspects of diversity and representation does it address, and why is this representation needed in your classroom? *Refer to tools in Chapter 3.*	This text contains respectful representations of physical dis/abilities and Asian characters. Specifically, it addresses the challenges a student with cerebral palsy faces when participating in school and making friends. While none of my students have cerebral palsy or a physical dis/ability, there are students with physical dis/abilities in our school. Representation of physical dis/abilities and differences is needed in my classroom because it can help my students see that people with physical differences are capable of doing many things and may share characteristics with Yipei.
Criticality Objective: How will you use the text to engage your students' thinking about representation, power, equity, and anti-oppression in this mini-lesson? (*Adapted from Muhammad, 2020*)	People with physical differences are as smart and capable as everyone else. In fact, they often have to work harder and be smarter to overcome differences, as Yipei does.
Common Core State Standard	RL.3.3 Describe characters in a story (e.g., their traits, motivations, or feelings) and explain how their actions contribute to the sequence of events.
ELA Learning Objective	Students will be able to use evidence from the text to describe the main character, Yipei.

Opening/ Hook	Today we are going to use evidence from the text to describe the main character from this beautiful book, *Woodpecker Girl*. This is a very special book because it tells the true story of a young girl from China who has a physical dis/ability, but overcomes it and learns to paint beautifully. Let's see what we can learn from the text about Yipei …
Modeling	Think aloud (page starts, "Mom was right."): Wow, Yipei described so many challenges she had and so many things that she wanted to do but couldn't. Then, she said she decided to change and started talking to her classmates through a computer and she has some friends now. I'm thinking that overcoming all those challenges took a lot of hard work. Yipei said, "I tried to change," and I think she worked really hard to make friends. At this point, I think Yipei is a very hard worker.
Guided Learning	(Page starts, "The headband felt uncomfortable …") On this page, Yipei says the headband is uncomfortable and it is exhausting to paint using the headband. But she also said she was, "… spreading [her] wings and flying freely in the sky." Turn and tell your partner what you think this page is saying about Yipei. Can she feel uncomfortable and free at the same time? What are we learning about her? (Page starts, "I follow the shining stars and fly home …") Yipei has been telling us how she has been flying like a woodpecker and what she has been seeing. But we know she can't really fly. What is Yipei saying? What are we learning about her as we look at her paintings? Turn and talk to your partner.
Independent Practice	(Second-to-last page starts, "I love painting.") Yipei says she has to paint slowly, dot-by-dot, and it makes her neck sore. But she also says she loves it. What does that tell us about Yipei? Write one or two words that you think describe Yipei on your whiteboard and then we'll share. I will write all your words down on our class whiteboard so we have a class list.
Closure	Thank you for sharing words that describe Yipei. Now, let's use these words to create a short poem to describe Yipei. Let's make sure to include evidence from the story in our poem. This poem is called an Acrostic Poem. Sample Acrostic Poem using the words *girl, doesn't give up, exhausted/tired, paint*: Young girl Imaginative, dreams of flying like a woodpecker Persistent, doesn't give up Exhausted, paints dot-by-dot Inspiring
Assessment	Exit Ticket: Choose one of the words on our class list that describe Yipei. What evidence from the book tells you that she is ____? (How do you know?)

CHAPTER 4 | How Do I Use Diverse Texts Across My Literacy Block?

> **Read this!**
>
> Muhammad, G. (2020). *Cultivating genius: An equity framework for culturally and historically responsive literacy.* Scholastic Inc. While Muhammad's book focuses on the teaching of Black youth, the ideas apply across different groups of people.

Let Students Choose

Before we continue to highlight the parts of your reading block where you can incorporate the use of diverse texts, we want to take a moment to discuss student choice. With so many mandates, district targets, and assessments, and only about six and a half hours in the average school day (minus drop-off, lunch, dismissal, etc.), it is incredibly easy for student choice to evaporate. But this is a mistake and works against the aspirational goals you have for your students. As we will show, there are several reasons to use student choice to enhance your instruction and elevate diversity.

The Benefits of Choice

First is the engagement factor. Providing opportunities for students to self-select books enables them to literally choose their own adventure. Students may choose to read about characters with whom they can personally relate, or they may choose to read about different cultures and lived experiences. They may choose to develop interests in insects, dinosaurs, or fashion, or they may choose to read all the books ever written by their favorite author. Regardless, this joyful time of independent reading for students supports their identity development, as they learn different ways of relating to characters, peers, and school adults (Francois, 2013).

Second, student choice is particularly important for students who are described as "disengaged" or "reluctant readers." While we believe that "No child is born a reluctant reader" (Goodwin, 2017, p. 33), our schools can turn children into reluctant learners when we privilege certain backgrounds and devalue others. Self-selecting books provides time and space for students who may not normally see themselves represented in the curriculum to find books that reflect and interest them. Having a wide variety of genres, topics, and characters represented in your classroom is particularly important for underserved students. In fact, a meta-analysis found that the two most powerful things teachers could do to improve reading motivation and comprehension were: (1) provide students access to many books, and (2) support personal choice of what to read (Guthrie & Humenick, 2004).

Third, students who choose their own books tend to read more, and those who read more tend to understand more. Choice elevates students' motivation to read and also helps them become better at selecting texts they are able to read well, resulting in improved comprehension (Allington & Gabriel, 2012). If students initially have trouble choosing texts that match their ability level and interest, you can help guide them. Learning to choose appropriate texts for themselves also significantly increases the likelihood students will read outside school (Ivey & Broaddus, 2001; Reis et al., 2007).

> "Self-selecting books provides time and space for students who may not normally see themselves represented in the curriculum to find books that reflect and interest them."

> **Quick Tip**
> Be careful not to make decisions for your library based only on what you like to read. Having a wide range of books provides multiple options for other types of readers to engage.

We understand that gathering an abundance of diverse texts can be difficult. Budgets are tight and few teachers earn sufficient salaries to ease the burden. However, technology is making it easier. There are many apps that schools subscribe to. The library app, Libby, provides free access to e-books and audiobooks. In addition, we share a number of strategies for acquiring hard copies of books inexpensively in Chapter 3, such as from garage and library sales, online resources, or from family, friends, and colleagues.

Last, we want to share a final note about choice. While focusing on providing students with more agency for the books they select, it is important that you do not fall into the trap of limiting students' access to certain levels of books. While there may be a time and place for leveled texts, student choice is paramount. High interest is a great motivator and can frequently help students surpass what their assessments show. If a book is too difficult, a child should be able to identify it for themselves and select another book that they will enjoy more—keeping the locus of control in their hands. Holding what you've read here about choice in mind, let's return to the remaining parts of the literacy block.

> "While there may be a time and place for leveled texts, student choice is paramount. High interest is a great motivator and can frequently help students surpass what their assessments show."

Book Talks, Book Clubs, Conferring, and More...

Small groups are one opportunity for students to engage in critical thought and conversations about diverse texts.

There are several opportunities for students to discuss self-selected texts throughout the literacy block. These moments often occur in small groups or when teachers are conferring with students one on one. The instructional moves outlined below keep students engaged in critical thought and conversations about diverse texts throughout the day.

Book Talks

How can you help children who do not know what types of books they like to read? Try connecting it back to the things they like to do or the types of media they consume. Do they like to watch cartoons where a mystery is solved? Try a mystery. Do they like to play basketball video games? You could try suggesting a book about LeBron James. You can also suggest that they get book recommendations from other students in the class who also like to play a particular video game, sport, or have a particular interest.

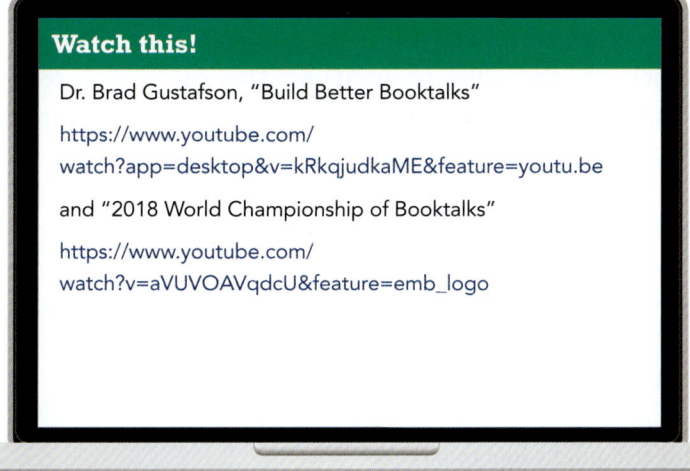

Watch this!

Dr. Brad Gustafson, "Build Better Booktalks"

https://www.youtube.com/watch?app=desktop&v=kRkqjudkaME&feature=youtu.be

and "2018 World Championship of Booktalks"

https://www.youtube.com/watch?v=aVUVOAVqdcU&feature=emb_logo

CHAPTER 4 | How Do I Use Diverse Texts Across My Literacy Block?

A book talk is a brief sales pitch, given by you or a student, to generate interest for independent reading time.

Book talks are a great strategy to introduce books to your students and get them excited. A book talk is essentially a brief sales pitch for a book intended to generate interest for independent reading time. It provides students with ideas about which books they might want to select. You can also teach students how to give book talks; it can be a structure they use to share their favorite books with one another.

Book talks motivate students to try out new books. They are generally done orally and are no more than three minutes long. While there isn't a right or wrong way to do book talks, Dr. Brad Gustafson provides one way in his YouTube video "Build Better Booktalks." He describes that the book talk should include the acronym HEAT:

- **Hook** – State why it's exciting, interesting, or why your students might like it. This is similar to a hook in a piece of writing and may also be posed as a question.

- **Energy** – Describe what you liked about it.

- **Audience** – Connect the text to students' lives to explain what they will learn by reading it.

- **Time** – Practice to keep the book talk brief, under 60 seconds, highlighting key information.

In order to deepen the social justice focus of your book talks, we suggest including the following questions. They can be included in the "Energy" and/or "Audience" sections. Some suggestions for the primary grades include:

- What does this book remind you of?

- How does this book make you feel about yourself or your family?

- What characters did you connect with? Why?

- Who else might like this book? Why?

Some of the following questions might be more appropriate for upper-grade students:

- Who are the main characters and how did you connect with them (or not)? (For example, mirror, window, or sliding glass door.)

- Whose perspective is heard? Whose is absent or silenced?

- What connections can you make between the book and our community or current events?

- What did you appreciate about this book?

Sample Book Talks

Feel free to adapt these questions for your context and the age and maturity of your students. Below is a sample book talk given by me (Allison) to a class of second graders. It is for Matt de la Peña's *Carmela Full of Wishes* (2018).

> Do you have a brother or sister that you argue with a lot? I do. My sister and I always argued when we were kids. In *Carmela Full of Wishes*, it's Carmela's birthday and she is finally old enough to hang out with her brother all day as he does errands for the family. The story is told from Carmela's perspective. I connected to Carmela like she was a mirror when she was arguing with her brother, but the book was also a sliding glass door for me, because in one spot I learned that her father was having immigration issues. I wanted to know more about that. I strongly recommend this book to anyone who is looking for a good story about a family. It's *Carmela Full of Wishes*, written by Matt de la Peña and illustrated by Christian Robinson.

CHAPTER 4 | **How Do I Use Diverse Texts Across My Literacy Block?**

Many students may be familiar with canonical stories like *Cinderella* or *The Little Red Hen*. We can relate diverse texts to familiar stories to garner students' interests. For example, you might tell students:

> If you like *Little Red Riding Hood*, you'll also like *Lon Po Po: A Red-Riding Hood Story from China*. Similar to *Little Red Riding Hood*, the main character in *Lon Po Po* is a sneaky wolf who pretends to be three girls' Po Po, or grandmother, so they will let him inside the house and he can eat them. But the girls are clever and trick the wolf! You'll have to read it to see how they outsmart the wolf. *Lon Po Po: A Red-Riding Hood Story from China* is translated and illustrated by Ed Young. Young grew up in China and now lives in New York.

Students can get quite involved in a series! If you introduce one book in the series, you may want to tempt students to read the other as well. Remember, the goal is to generate interest and create enthusiasm for reading. Therefore, there aren't necessarily "right" or "wrong" ways to do book talks. Feel free to get creative and do what works for you and your students.

Book talks are a great way to introduce new books or book series to students with the goal of generating enthusiasm for reading.

Conferring

When we confer with a student, we have a genuine conversation about their reading and identity as a reader. Conferring provides an opportunity to individually assess exactly what students need, in the moment. It helps students connect our instruction to their reading, as they immediately get to apply skills that are discussed.

Conferences should be conversational, with the student usually talking more than you as they share their understandings about a text. Conferences can take many directions, based on the student's needs. We suggest taking a social justice approach to some of your conferring conversations. For example, a conference with a first grader about *Carmela Full of Wishes* might go something like this:

Teacher:	Good morning, Anaya, how is it going with your book today?
Anaya:	Good.
Teacher:	Tell me about it.
Anaya:	It's Carmela's birthday, and she had candles in her pancakes! My mom doesn't do that. I want that next time it's my birthday. I'm going to be 7.
Teacher:	And did Carmela make a birthday wish when she blew out the candles?
Anaya:	Yes, and then she makes more wishes! She picks dandelions and makes lots of wishes. But it doesn't say what she wished for.
Teacher:	What do you think she might have wished for?
Anaya:	Maybe that her brother would be nicer to her? Or that her dad would come home. It says he's not home, but I don't know why.
Teacher:	Let's go to that page and see what the author says. It says Carmela was "imagining her dad getting his papers fixed so he could finally be home." What might that mean?

CHAPTER 4 | How Do I Use Diverse Texts Across My Literacy Block?

Conferences can take many directions, based on students' needs.

Notice that this is an authentic, if brief, conversation about the book. Anaya makes connections to her own birthday, shows what she understands about the book, and also identifies what she does not understand. Anaya has been taught to self-monitor her comprehension so that she is able to recognize when she needs to think more or ask questions about a particular part of a book. This brief snippet of a conference opens up space for a deeper conversation about why Carmela's father is not able to be with the family and how upsetting that might be.

We suggest prompting readers with questions that allow for deeper discussions about race, power, and privilege during your conferences, such as:

- Who are the main characters and how did you connect with them (or not)? (For example, mirror, window, sliding glass door.)

- Whose perspective is heard? Whose is absent or silenced?

- What connections can you make between the book and our community or current events?

Comprehension questions that are oriented toward social justice will help students consider concepts like perspective, power, and privilege when reading on their own. Your questions become the students' inner voice, as they learn to take on a critical lens while reading. The deeper thinking will help them develop their own identities, as well as better understand the world around them.

> "Comprehension questions that are oriented toward social justice will help students consider concepts like perspective, power, and privilege when reading on their own."

Whole-Group Share

As you create a community of readers and writers in your classroom, you'll want to give students opportunities to talk about their own reading and writing. One opportunity to do that is after independent reading time in a whole-class setting. Traditionally, students may share anything from how they used a particular word-solving or comprehension strategy to a summary of a book they read for their peers. You, in collaboration with your students, can set the expectation for how this time is used. We suggest consistently incorporating prompts from the Conferring or Book Talks sections. Having these prompts tie back to your reading conferences and other social justice conversations with students in whole-group and small-group settings will support students' critical thinking and enable them to consider these important questions independently.

Book clubs support students' agency as they collaborate with peers in meaningful ways that deepen their understanding of a text.

Book Clubs

Book clubs, also known as literature circles, enable students to have choice in what they read and to collaborate with peers in ways that deepen their understanding of a text. Book clubs should be used when students are fairly proficient readers—meaning that they are able to independently read early chapter books—and can be used from second grade through adulthood with different levels of scaffolding and sophistication.

To participate in book clubs, small groups of students select one book from a variety of texts that are appropriate for their current reading ability. Earlier we shared how giving students choice increases engagement, motivation, and comprehension. Using diverse texts goes one step further to engage students whose identities are generally excluded from literacy practices. Students who are not accustomed to seeing themselves in books will have the opportunity to do so, as well as have the chance to learn about people who are different from them. Engaging students through choice and high-interest books increases their willingness and ability to access text.

CHAPTER 4 | How Do I Use Diverse Texts Across My Literacy Block?

> **Quick Tip**
>
> Book clubs can be used to address all of the elementary grade standards for reading fiction and informational texts. Since students will be working independently, teachers should consider keeping the task or the text at an independent reading level to avoid frustration.

While there is relative homogeneity in reading level within a book club group, having students with diversity of thought and backgrounds in the same group can help build relationships among diverse students.

In the beginning, it is important to scaffold the discussion. Book club roles should be explicitly taught and reviewed before students are asked to complete them independently. You may choose to work with a small group to prepare a fish bowl model for other groups showing what a book club might look and sound like.

There are many options for book club roles, and roles may vary depending on students' ages, their strengths and challenges, the type of text, the number of students in a group, and other factors. Students either select or are given roles, and then prepare based on those roles. The original book club roles came from research on reciprocal teaching (Palincsar & Brown, 1984) and included questioner, clarifier/word detective, predictor, and summarizer.

> "Having students with diversity of thought and backgrounds in the same group can help build relationships among diverse students."

We suggest adding new roles* that help students connect the text to their lives and communities. For example:

- **Representation Rep** – identifies who is represented and who is missing from the text. This person considers whose voice is heard and whose is silenced or marginalized.

- **Perspective Taker** – identifies whose perspective is being represented and explains what that perspective is. This person intentionally takes the perspectives of others and contrasts them with the narrator's (or narrators') perspective.

- **Community Connector** – makes connections among the selected text, other texts, personal experiences, the lived experiences of those in the community, and current events. This person finds relevance and relationships between the text and students' lives.

- **Stereotype Seeker** – looks for and calls out stereotypes, tokenism, and other inauthentic representations of diversity.

You should join the group's discussion at first, but gradually shift the group to independence. You may also listen in to assess participation and understanding. Independent student work related to the book, such as written or video responses to the text, can also be used to assess individuals' comprehension.

See the reproducible role cards in English and Spanish at the end of this chapter.

> **Quick Tip**
>
> Certain publishers pay more attention to diversity and representation. Publishers such as Reycraft Books, Flamingo Rampant, Row House Publishing, and Lee & Low Books specialize in diverse texts.

Writing

Similarly, diverse texts can be the basis for many of the writing standards. For example, the second-grade standard 2.1 states:

> Write opinion pieces in which they introduce the topic or book they are writing about, state an opinion, supply reasons that support the opinion, use linking words (e.g., *because*, *and*, *also*) to connect opinion and reasons, and provide a concluding statement, or section.

A text such as *The Legend of the Coquí* (2020) by Georgina Lázaro, can be used to address this standard. A legend from Puerto Rico, the book ends with the lesson, "Remember that you have a voice, too. And even if you are little, you can still do big things."

Common Core State Standard	2.1 (*see above*)
Mini-Lesson Objective	Students will be able to write an opinion and provide two reasons that support the opinion.
Writing Task: Possibility A	Do you agree or disagree that individuals of small stature can do big things? In one paragraph, state your opinion and provide two reasons that support your opinion. You may choose to include examples if you'd like.
Writing Task: Possibility B	The frogs that won the race did not have the strength or speed that other animals have. Do you think a group of people can achieve something when they work together even if they are not the most powerful? In one paragraph, state your opinion and provide two reasons that support your opinion. You may choose to include examples if you'd like.

In this instance, the book represents Puerto Rican culture, but Writing Task A is somewhat unrelated to issues of diversity. You can choose to elevate the social justice level by using a different book or changing the task, for example, to Writing Task B.

Just like the messages of different books are on a continuum from representation to advocacy (see Chapter 3), the tasks you ask students to do in response to texts can also be on a continuum of social justice action. We talk more about this in Chapter 5.

> "Just like the messages of different books are on a continuum from representation to advocacy, [so are] the tasks you ask students to do in response."

You can elevate the social justice level of a thematic unit by the text(s) you select and/or the task(s) students complete in response.

Tools to Try

This chapter's tools are designed to help you share diverse texts with students. The lesson plan template is a support for you during the planning stage, as thinking through the lesson and the diverse text in advance will help the lesson go smoothly. The prompting cards are scaffolds for students during small-group conversations. We provide a Spanish translation of the prompting cards for Spanish/English bilingual settings or as support for Spanish-literate students in English monolingual settings.

Tool 4.1 Using Diverse Texts Lesson Plan Template

This tool is designed to help you get started using diverse texts with your students. It starts by asking you to consider what you learned about your students using Tool 2.1. It prompts you to articulate a rationale for the diverse text you have selected. A space to reflect on the criticality objective will help you ensure your students engage in deep, critical thinking about representation, power, equity and anti-oppression. Content objective and other fields help you with planning a comprehensive and effective lesson.

Careful planning helps you ensure that students engage in deep, critical thinking about representation, power, equity, and anti-oppression.

Tool 4.1 Using Diverse Texts Lesson Plan Template

Lesson Title:	**Grade Level:**
Teacher Name:	Anticipated Time/Length:
Student Identities: Use the results from Tool 2.1 to draft a list of your students' identities here. (*Adapted from Muhammad, 2020*)	
Diverse Text Title and Author	
Diverse Text Rationale: Why did you select this diverse text? What aspects of diversity and representation does it address, and why is this representation needed in your classroom? *Refer to Tool 1.1 and the tools in Chapter 3.*	
Criticality Objective: How will you use the text to engage your students' thinking about representation, power, equity, and anti-oppression in this mini-lesson? (*Adapted from Muhammad, 2020*)	
Common Core State Standard	
ELA Learning Objective	
Opening/Hook	
Modeling	
Guided Learning	
Independent Practice	
Closure	
Assessment of Criticality Objective and ELA Learning Objective	

CHAPTER 4 | How Do I Use Diverse Texts Across My Literacy Block?

Tool 4.2 Prompting Cards for New Book Club Roles

Use prompting cards to help students get more out of book clubs. These social justice prompting cards identify four new roles: Representation Rep, Perspective Taker, Community Connector, and Stereotype Seeker. They also list important questions and prompts for students in each role to consider. Using these cards will help students learn to ask hard questions, challenge other students' thinking, and be critical of the text. We provide a Spanish translation of the cards in Tool 4.2b.

Looking Ahead

- **Chapter 5** tools help you incorporate diverse texts across the curriculum.

- **Chapter 6** tools help you and your students assess and reflect on progress.

Tool 4.2a Prompting Cards for New Book Club Roles

Representation Rep
- Who is represented in this book?
- Who is not represented?
- Who gets to tell this story? Why?
- Do you notice any characters being silenced? How and by whom?
- Are there any characters you would like to hear more from or know more about?

Perspective Taker
- I noticed that _____ perspective dominates this book. What do you think about that?
- I wonder how the story would change if it were told from _____'s perspective?
- Who else might have an important opinion or perspective in this book? What might it be?

Community Connector
- Who has a personal connection to the events or the characters they would like to share? How does it help you understand this text?
- Are there any connections between this book and current events? How does that help you understand the book or the current events differently?
- How can we relate this book to our community? What can we learn about the book or the community from the connection we made?

Stereotype Seeker
- Are there any stereotypes, or representations of people as "typical" for a group?
- Do women, people of color, and other minoritized characters have agency? Or are they tokenized?
- Do characters lose out when compared with White middle class as the "standard"?
- Who are the heroes? The villains?

Tool 4.2b Tarjetas para Animar Participación: Tarjetas de pautas para nuevos roles

Animar la representación
- ¿Quién está representado en este libro?
- ¿Quién no está representado?
- ¿Quién cuenta esta historia? ¿Por qué?
- ¿Notas que algunos personajes no se "escuchan"? ¿Cómo y por quién?
- ¿Hay algún personaje del que te gustaría saber más o sobre el que te gustaría saber más?

Tomar otra perspectiva
- Noté que la perspectiva de _____ domina este libro. ¿Qué piensas sobre eso?
- Me pregunto cómo cambiaría la historia si se contara desde la perspectiva de _____.
- ¿Quién más podría tener una opinión o perspectiva importante en este libro? ¿Qué podría ser?

Conectar a la comunidad
- ¿Quién tiene una conexión personal con los eventos o los personajes que les gustaría compartir? ¿Cómo los ayuda a entender este texto?
- ¿Existe alguna conexión entre este libro y los eventos actuales? ¿Cómo te ayuda eso a entender el libro o los eventos actuales de manera diferente?
- ¿Cómo podemos relacionar este libro con nuestra comunidad? ¿Qué podemos aprender sobre el libro o la comunidad de la conexión que hicimos?

Buscar estereotipos
- ¿Existen estereotipos o representaciones de personas "típicas" de un grupo?
- ¿Tienen libre albedrio las mujeres, personas de color y otros personajes minoritarios? ¿O son personajes simbólicos?
- ¿Salen perdiendo estos personajes cuando se comparan con las clase media blanca como "estándar"?
- ¿Quiénes son los héroes? ¿Quiénes son villanos?

Voices from the Field

Claire Hood
teacher

"The more you [use diverse texts], the more comfortable you feel."

An experienced White teacher in Santa Clara Unified School District in California, Claire Hood has taught kindergarten, second, and fifth grades. When asked if she ever gets nervous about using diverse texts with her students, she laughed and replied, "I have this conversation with student teachers a lot when they come to observe me to see how I use diverse texts. I explain to them, 'The more you [use diverse texts], the more comfortable you feel. And it's really deciding, what kind of conversations do I want kids to be able to have? Do I want them to not be able to talk about diverse texts? Or do I want to pretend they're not experiencing the issues that they're experiencing?'"

For Claire, gay rights have always been the hardest topic to bring into the classroom because she wants to be respectful of all people's beliefs. She said, "But I finally decided, you know, I can't ignore it. And not talking about it isn't benefiting my students. What is the worst thing that can happen to me for reading a book that is teaching historically about Stonewall or Harvey Milk?" In fact, Claire's students became very engaged in conversations about the gay rights movement. She explained, "So, for example, with reading and studying Harvey Milk, we had such great conversations that my kids wanted to read more. And then we read about Stonewall and talked about transgender rights."

She added, "We got a little bit more into sexuality than I was ready for. But my fifth graders were ready for it. We were having these conversations because they were interested." She explained, "As long as you're letting them lead it, and making sure that you're facilitating the conversation in a way that respects all students, then it's worth it."

Claire continued, "I think a lot of [teachers] just don't know where to start" because of the perception that certain topics are taboo. Despite this, however, she believes "It is our job to be social justice leaders. And we have the ability to make an impact on our communities."

"It is our job to be social justice leaders. And we have the ability to make an impact on our communities."

Voices from the Field

Cecilia Carrillo
teacher

"I need to make sure I use books that are related to my students' lives."

Cecilia Carrillo is a bilingual Mexican American fifth-grade teacher in Milpitas Unified School District in Milpitas, California. She has taught for three years, using diverse texts in read-alouds, book clubs, and independent reading activities. Cecilia engages students in read-alouds using diverse texts that reflect a wide range of values she would like her students to explore. She explains, "The first word I teach at the beginning of the school year is the word 'respect.' I use different books to teach different words across the school year that help my students become more successful and increase their self-esteem." She selects diverse texts for book clubs and asks small groups to discuss their culture and what they like and dislike. At the end, each group delivers a presentation where they teach the whole class about the text.

Cecilia has been growing her classroom library and makes sure she has diverse texts that will engage her students as they read independently. "When they finish reading the book," she says, "they present it to our classroom." She explains, "They create a graphic organizer with the book title and the characters on the left. And then they add the main idea and the ultimate message of the book." She adds, "I also like to hold events with guests and motivational speakers from different backgrounds. Parents are invited to come to our classroom and they teach us how to cook a dish from their culture. And through that, I prepare my students to read texts from that culture."

Cecilia works to link reading and writing across the school year by having students stop, reflect, and write about what they're reading. She incorporates diverse texts, like *Esperanza Rising*, in her social studies instruction by making connections to the historical time period and geographical references.

Her use of diverse texts to supplement the adopted curriculum has caught the attention of administrators. She shared, "They sent me an email asking, 'Can you explain why you are using or reading this book?' And then I show that, with this book, I am teaching all the reading strategies, which is finding main ideas, cause and effect, challenges the characters face, and then how the character overcomes the challenge. And at the same time, I'm teaching social-emotional learning by using books that are related to my students' lives. Some kids are living with foster parents and other kids are facing other challenges at home. For me, it is very important to focus on social-emotional learning because if students don't feel comfortable in my classroom or know that I care, they're not going to care about learning."

Using diverse texts throughout the school day and focusing on students' social-emotional learning has helped Cecilia build trust and community in her classroom. This helps the class focus on learning instead of struggling with classroom management issues. Cecilia reflects, "I see that some new teachers struggle with classroom management. They build these discipline strategies, but they don't need to if trust is built with the students and teacher."

Cecilia also calls home to boast about her students' great behavior and accomplishments. She asks students to make a list of the things they did right in school that week and she calls home with the good news.

CHAPTER 5 | How Do I Use Diverse Texts Across the Content Areas?

How Do I Use Diverse Texts Across the Content Areas?

CHAPTER 5

Big Idea

Integrating diverse texts across the curriculum builds background knowledge, supports student engagement, and enables students to connect to and access content differently.

The beauty of diverse texts is that they cover just about any topic and genre you can imagine. Therefore, these books can be used to amplify content in social studies, math, and science without sacrificing other core standards. The key is to position them in units in the right way to help students build background knowledge, make connections, or access information differently.

Using diverse texts also helps you integrate different content areas. For example, a book about a Mexican inventor that you use during your reading block can be revisited in science to show the real-world implications of a particular scientific skill. The same text will also underscore that people who are not from the United States, and may not speak English, are also major contributors to world improvement. This illustration is only a snippet of the far-reaching benefits of using diverse texts throughout your day. We promise that the outcomes are well worth the investment.

This chapter begins with social studies, the most common content connection. Then, we show how to incorporate diverse texts into math and science content. The end of the chapter contains a tool for outlining social justice units that incorporate diverse texts.

CHAPTER 5 | How Do I Use Diverse Texts Across the Content Areas?

> **Read this!**
> Colwell, J. (2019). Selecting texts for disciplinary literacy instruction. *The Reading Teacher, 72*(5), 631–637. This article helps you select texts for cross-curricular units with a Disciplinary Text Selection Table.

Social Studies

The integration of diverse texts with social studies standards and curriculum is a natural fit. There are many historical fiction texts that could be used alongside primary source materials or social studies textbooks. Of course, there are also many children's books that are biographies written about important historical figures. For example, Harvey Milk, a gay rights activist and the first openly gay elected official in California, is an important figure who does not always make it into the social studies curriculum. California state history is traditionally taught in fourth grade; it is easy to incorporate his story into the curriculum through the children's book *Pride: The Story of Harvey Milk and the Rainbow Flag* (2018) by Rob Sanders. This book can also be used to teach any of the following Grades 6–8 ELA/Social Studies Common Core State Standards, among others:

Standards Aligned to *Pride: The Story of Harvey Milk and the Rainbow Flag* by Rob Sanders

> **Standard 1:** Cite specific textual evidence to support analysis of primary and secondary sources.
>
> **Standard 5:** Describe how a text presents information (e.g., sequentially, comparatively, causally).
>
> **Standard 6:** Identify aspects of a text that reveal an author's point of view or purpose (e.g., loaded language, inclusion or avoidance of particular facts).

Natural Allies

The integration of social studies with diverse texts is important because the two complement each other so well. For instance, diverse texts help students better comprehend the struggles of a given time period and the individuals who made an impact. Similarly, social studies content provides students with a deeper understanding of the context, culture, and epoch of the diverse books, so the learning is reciprocal. The sample immigration unit later in this chapter provides an example of how diverse texts could be integrated across a social studies unit. On the following page, you will see a chart of suggested diverse texts to enhance social studies curriculum.

> **Quick Tip**
>
> As you work on your classroom library audit (Tools 1.1 and 1.2), you may want to take note of books that can fit into the various content areas.

"Diverse texts help students better comprehend the struggles of a given time period and the individuals who made an impact."

Social studies content provides deeper understanding of the context and culture surrounding diverse books.

CHAPTER 5 | How Do I Use Diverse Texts Across the Content Areas?

Diverse Texts That Support Social Studies

Title	Grade Levels	Related Social Studies Unit(s)
The Bracelet by Yoshiko Uchida	K–2	World War II, internment camps, Asian American history
Baseball Saved Us by Ken Mochizuki	K–2	World War II, internment camps, Asian American history
Pride: The Story of Harvey Milk and the Rainbow Flag by Rob Sanders	K–5	California history, civil rights (LGBTQ)
All the Way to the Top: How One Girl's Fight for Americans with Disabilities Changed Everything by Annette Bay Pimentel	K–2	dis/ability rights movement, civil rights
When I Was Eight by Christy Jordan-Fenton and Margaret Pokiak-Fenton	1–4	Native American history
Let It Shine: Stories of Black Women Freedom Fighters by Andrea Davis Pinkney	1–4	African American history, women's rights, civil rights
Separate Is Never Equal: Sylvia Mendez and Her Family's Fight for Desegregation by Duncan Tonatiuh	1–4	Latinx people's history, civil rights
William Still and His Freedom Stories: The Father of the Underground Railroad by Don Tate	1–5	African American history, Underground Railroad, civil rights
We Are Still Here!: Native American Truths Everyone Should Know by Traci Sorell	3–5	Native American history, civil rights
Mary and the Trail of Tears: A Cherokee Removal Survival Story by Andrea L. Rogers	3–5	Native American history, Trail of Tears

Math

Recently, a number of children's books have been published that show the diversity of people who have made significant contributions in math and science, including women, who have traditionally been marginalized in these fields. For example, *The Girl With a Mind for Math: The Story of Raye Montague* (2018) by Julia Finley Mosca tells of Montague's math expertise that led her to be the first person to design a military ship using computers in under 19 hours.

Similarly, *Counting on Katherine: How Katherine Johnson Saved Apollo 13* (2018) by Helaine Becker recounts how Black female mathematician Katherine Johnson influenced the Apollo 13 mission. *Counting on Katherine* is recommended for Grades 1 and 2 and includes multiple opportunities to launch into mathematics concepts aligned with Grades 1 and 2 CCSS. The first pages of the book, for example, share how Katherine loved to count all types of objects inside and outside her home. First graders can be encouraged to love counting, like Katherine, by walking outside the classroom to count trees, leaves under a particular tree, bicycles, jump ropes, or classrooms in a school building. Second graders can be invited to skip-count objects by 5s, 10s, and 100s. Students can also learn to plot numbers on a graph and ask and answer questions about the data, like Katherine. Below, we share a sample of Grades 1 and 2 CCSS math standards that can be easily aligned to the book *Counting on Katherine*.

Standards Aligned to *Counting on Katherine* by Helaine Becker

- CCSS.MATH.CONTENT.1.NBT.A.1 Count to 120, starting at any number less than 120. In this range, read and write numerals and represent a number of objects with a written numeral.
- CCSS.MATH.CONTENT.1.MD.C.4 Organize, represent, and interpret data with up to three categories; ask and answer questions about the total number of data points, how many in each category, and how many more or less are in one category than in another.
- CCSS.MATH.CONTENT.2.NBT.A.2 Count within 1000; skip-count by 5s, 10s, and 100s.
- CCSS.MATH.CONTENT.2.MD.D.9 Generate measurement data by measuring lengths of several objects to the nearest whole unit, or by making repeated measurements of the same object. Show the measurements by making a line plot, where the horizontal scale is marked off in whole-number units.

CHAPTER 5 | How Do I Use Diverse Texts Across the Content Areas?

Stories like *The Girl With a Mind for Math* and *Counting on Katherine* not only help students of color and women to see that they, too, have a place in mathematics, but they also aid students in understanding why the mathematics content is important and how they could contribute to society through mathematics.

There are also children's books that teach math concepts and include characters from communities who speak languages other than English. For example, Ana Crespo's *Lia & Luís: Who Has More?* (2020) is a story of Brazilian twins. The book, which includes Brazilian Portuguese words and references to Brazilian culture, tells the story of Luís, who always wants to have more of anything than his sister, Lia. Books like this teach math concepts while including diverse characters, showing that everyone can do math.

Diverse books aid students in understanding why mathematics content is important and that everyone can do math.

Science

Similar to math, there are an increasing number of books that highlight scientists of note who come from diverse backgrounds. For example, the adult book and movie *Hidden Figures* was made into a children's book, *Hidden Figures: The True Story of Four Black Women and the Space Race* (2018) by Margot Lee Shetterly. This book explores the story of four Black NASA scientists who overcame gender and racial barriers and significantly contributed to the first launching of humans into space.

Children's books are now also written about ordinary people who may not have formal scientific training but whose ideas impact the scientific and local communities. For example, *Iqbal and His Ingenious Idea: How a Science Project Helps One Family and the Planet* (2018) by Elizabeth Suneby is ideal for students in Grades 3 through 7. It recounts the story of a Bangladeshi Muslim boy, Iqbal, who devises a cookstove for his mother that does not produce smoke, solving a global health problem. When Iqbal learned about his school's science fair, he began to think about inventions that could help his family and community. He decided to build a stove that did not produce smoke because he wanted to help women like his mother be able to cook without breathing smoke from an indoor open fire. Iqbal defined a problem, and developed and used a model that would help solve the problem. These are two of eight scientific practices that make up the Next Generation Science Standards (NGSS).

Guided by the NGSS, students can come to see that, like Iqbal, they, too, can come up with scientific inventions that help people they care about. On the following page, we share a sample of NGSS standards that work well with the book *Iqbal and His Ingenious Idea*.

> **Quick Tip**
>
> Include books showing everyday people making changes in their community. This will help students see themselves as agents of change along with expanding the definition of *diversity*.

CHAPTER 5 | How Do I Use Diverse Texts Across the Content Areas?

> **Quick Tip**
>
> The NGSS supports the integration of literacy and science. In fact, Appendix M of the NGSS aligns the NGSS to the Common Core ELA standards, so that work is already done for you.

Some NGSS Standards Aligned to *Iqbal and His Ingenious Idea* by Elizabeth Suneby

- NGSS.3-PS2-4 Motion and Stability: Forces and Interactions - Define a simple design problem that can be solved by applying scientific ideas about magnets.
- NGSS.3-5-ETS1-1 Engineering Design - Define a simple design problem reflecting a need or a want that includes specified criteria for success and constraints on materials, time, or cost.
- NGSS.MS-ETS1-1 Engineering Design - Define the criteria and constraints of a design problem with sufficient precision to ensure a successful solution, taking into account relevant scientific principles and potential impacts on people and the natural environment that may limit possible solutions.

Books about everyday people from diverse backgrounds who apply science help students understand that they can contribute to solving community and global problems.

Similarly, *One Plastic Bag: Isatou Ceesay and the Recycling Women of the Gambia* (2015) by Miranda Paul tells of a Gambian woman who finds a way to recycle the plastic bags that were littering her town, killing livestock that tried to eat them, and interfering with agriculture. These inspiring stories show the impact that everyday people "doing" science can have on their communities.

There are also diverse books that teach science content and the significance of science in today's world. For example, *We Are Water Protectors* (2020) by Carole Lindstrom, an Ojibwe author, is inspired by the many Native-led movements to protect Earth. Its Native American characters explain the significance of water to a Native community and to our collective life. This 2021 winner of the Caldecott Medal could be easily used at a variety of grade levels during science units on water cycles, conservation, and climate change. On pages 128–129, you will see a sample science lesson plan based on the book, *Galimoto*, which recounts a tale from Malawi.

CHAPTER 5 | How Do I Use Diverse Texts Across the Content Areas?

A galimoto is a homemade toy vehicle.

Sample Science Lesson: *Galimoto* by Karen Lynn Williams

Although *Galimoto* (1990) by Karen Lynn Williams is an older book, it aligns well with the NGSS. In this tale from Malawi, the young Kondi uses his savvy to acquire enough wire to create his own galimoto, or toy vehicle, similar to what a student might do in a makerspace or other hands-on STEM setting. We used the lesson plan template from Chapter 4 (Tool 4.1) to incorporate *Galimoto* in a science lesson.

Lesson Title: Creating Bigger Things from Smaller Ones	Grade Level: 2
Teacher Name:	**Anticipated Time/Length:**
Student Identities: Use the results from Tool 2.1 to draft a list of your students' identities here. (*Adapted from Muhammad, 2020*)	• Bilingual - Arabic, Vietnamese • Student with autism • Vietnamese • Mexican American • Middle Eastern • Variety of religions
Diverse Text Title and Author	*Galimoto* by Karen Lynn Williams, illustrated by Catherine Stock
Diverse Text Rationale: Why did you select this diverse text? What aspects of diversity and representation does it address, and why is this representation needed in your classroom?	This story is about a Black boy from Malawi, Kondi, who collects wire from different places in his village and then creates a galimoto, or push toy vehicle. I chose this text because it shows a child of color building something from small parts.
Criticality Objective: How will you use the text to engage your students' thinking about representation, power, equity, and anti-oppression in this mini-lesson? (*Adapted from Muhammad, 2020*)	This text engages students' thinking of representation by highlighting Kondi, a Black boy, using his imagination and his community's resources to create something he can play with and that he can also adapt.
Standard	NGSS 2-PS1-3 Matter and Its Interactions: *Make observations to construct an evidence-based account of how an object made of a small set of pieces can be disassembled and made into a new object.*

Lesson Title: Creating Bigger Things from Smaller Ones	Grade Level: 2
Learning Objective	Students will learn that with imagination and small parts they can create new things.
Opening/Hook	Have you ever wanted a toy but didn't have it? This story is about a boy who found a way to make a toy he wanted by collecting small things from around his village in Malawi.
Modeling	Read *Galimoto* aloud to show how Kondi collects wire and makes a toy that he can then take apart to create something new the next day.
Guided Learning	Student pairs share and then discuss as a whole their responses to the question, "What did Kondi do to create his galimoto?"
Independent Practice	Provide students with various objects, such as magnets, small wheels, wire, twist ties, string, paper clips, and paper bags. Ask them to create something that can be used to move small classroom objects (e.g., erasers, pencils) from one end of the classroom to the other.
Closure	Students share their inventions, explaining the small parts they used and showing how their invention works. Teacher reinforces stated objective.
Assessment of Criticality Objective and Learning Objective	Rubric: • **Meets objective:** Student can explain how they used small parts to create something that can move things from one place to another, and the object works. • **Approaches objective:** Student can explain how they used small parts to create something that should be able to move things from one place to another; the invention may not work. • **Does not yet meet objective:** Student may be unable to explain how they used small parts to make their invention.

CHAPTER 5 | How Do I Use Diverse Texts Across the Content Areas?

> **Read this!**
>
> Brown, B. A. (2019). *Science in the city: Culturally relevant STEM education*. Harvard Education Press. This book illustrates how science education can flourish if it is connected to students' backgrounds, identities, language, and culture.

Diverse Texts That Support Math and Science

Below is a list of diverse texts that may be used to enhance math and science curricula.

Title	Grade Levels	Related Unit(s)
We Are Water Protectors by Carole Lindstrom	K–2	Science: environmental justice, environmental science, water cycle
Abby Invents Unbreakable Crayons by Arlyne Simon	K–3	Science: engineering, design, inventing, perseverance, women in STEM
One Step Further: My Story of Math, the Moon, and a Lifelong Mission by Katherine Johnson, Joylette Hylick, and Katherine Moore	K–3	Math: importance of math, becoming a mathematician, women in STEM
The World Is Not a Rectangle: A Portrait of Architect Zaha Hadid by Jeanette Winter	K–4	Math: shapes, geometry, women in STEM
Buzzing with Questions: The Inquisitive Mind of Charles Henry Turner by Janice N. Harrington	2–5	Science: biology, insects, life cycles
Girls Who Code by Stacia Deutsch	5–8	Math: importance of math, becoming a mathematician, women in STEM

Expanding the Conversation

When using diverse texts, it helps to know your students well. Students who have particular background knowledge or lived experience with a certain topic will have a comprehension advantage and a perspective to offer other students who have little to no personal connection to the topic. More often than not, this piques the interest of students who are less familiar with a topic, while offering students who are more familiar with it a platform from which to share their thoughts and experiences.

The comprehension conversations that result from using diverse texts may differ from the ones you are accustomed to. Students will connect to the texts in new or various ways as diverse perspectives are introduced and discussed. For example, *For All/Para Todos* by Alejandra Domenzain is a bilingual story about Flor and her father's journey from Mexico to the United States as undocumented immigrants. Flor is excited to make the journey to the land that is said to be "for all" and looks forward to living a life where her family has enough food and clothing. Once Flor and her father arrive in the United States, however, their life as undocumented immigrants is very different from what Flor imagined. This text highlights the challenges of undocumented immigrants living with the constant threat of deportation and struggling financially to make ends meet.

> "Students will connect to the texts in new or various ways as diverse perspectives are introduced and discussed."

CHAPTER 5 | How Do I Use Diverse Texts Across the Content Areas?

Discussion encourages students to value and respect one another's cultural and background differences.

Students with varying upbringings may have different reactions to the issues related to immigration and social class raised in this text, such as working long hours but not having enough money to pay for basic necessities. Prior experiences with caregivers working long hours and immigration family stories often arise in conversation. Students with this background knowledge might comprehend the text more easily, as it might be a mirror that reflects their lived experiences. Students from wealthier families or with no United States documentation concerns might have fewer personal connections to this book, and therefore greater difficulty comprehending. *For All/Para Todos*, therefore, might serve as a window for them to look into a life with immigration and socioeconomic challenges different from their own.

In summary, comprehension discussions can be deepened by engaging students' background knowledge. When misunderstandings occur, the student who has a lived experience with the topic can clarify rather than the teacher. If students have differing lived experiences, this opens the door to even more nuanced understanding. In this way, students' differences are explicitly valued in the classroom, and students come to value and respect one another's cultural differences. Importantly, since the teacher may not be present during small-group conversations, it is critical that students are taught how to engage in respectful conversations about differences. Chapter 6 has ideas for preparing students for respectful small-group discussions.

> "If students have differing lived experiences, this opens the door to even more nuanced understanding. In this way, students' differences are explicitly valued in the classroom."

Planning a Unit for Justice

Dr. Bree Picower, a Professor at Montclair State University in the College of Education and Human Development, identifies a progression of six elements to guide a social justice curriculum. This framework begins with "Self-Love and Knowledge" and "Respect for Others," where a topic is introduced in a respectful and caring way. The next sections, "Issues of Social Injustice" and "Social Movements and Social Change," are then used to explore how diversity can be experienced as oppression and how key figures and organizations mobilize to effect change. The final two sections, "Awareness Raising" and "Social Action," shift students into action. Here students brainstorm ways to actively engage in advocacy for the issue at hand.

Developing all six elements enables students to develop tools for analysis of oppression and for social action (Picower, 2012). We have adapted Picower's framework into a unit-planning template (Tool 5.1) to help you identify where different aspects of your curriculum land on the social justice scale so that you can adapt as you see fit. For example, some of the *representation* books, such as *King for a Day* and *Carmela Full of Wishes* (discussed in Chapter 3) might fall into the first two categories, "Self-Love and Knowledge" and "Respect for Others." However, either book could also be used further down the progression, depending on the instruction.

Plotting your curriculum on this scale can help you identify how far you are currently moving along the social justice teaching continuum. It can also help you identify your comfort zone. Many teachers feel quite comfortable with the first and second steps, "Self-Love and Knowledge" and "Respect for Others"—but can you push yourself further? For example, can you add new forms of diversity? If not, you're not alone. Chapter 6 explicitly addresses some common fears we have observed in teachers and ways to address them.

On pages 134–137, you will see a Grade 3 immigration unit based on this progression. We draw on easily accessible texts and a free video from the Learning for Justice website. We've included California History/Social Science Content Standards, but these can be adapted to meet your state's standards.

Sample Grade 3 Immigration Unit for Advancing Justice

Social Justice Element	Possible Texts
1. Self-Love and Knowledge • Teachers provide opportunities for students to learn who they are and where they come from. • Students study different aspects of their identities and associated histories. • Negative stereotypes about student identities are deconstructed.	*Dreamers* by Yuyi Morales tells the story of a woman and her infant immigrating to the U.S. *Carmela Full of Wishes* by Matt de la Peña is the story of a day in the life of an immigrant child, normalizing and problematizing the family's situation.
2. Respect for Others • Teachers provide students with opportunities to share knowledge about their own cultural background with their classmates. • A climate of respect for diversity is created through students' learning to listen with kindness and empathy to the experiences of their peers. • Students deconstruct stereotypes about their peers' identities.	*Carmela Full of Wishes* and *Dreamers* contrasted with a book that uses stereotypes of Latinx families, such as *Chato's Kitchen* (1997) by Gary Soto or *Skippyjon Jones* (2005) by Judy Schachner.
3. Issues of Social Injustice • Teachers move from celebrating diversity to an exploration of how diversity can be experienced as oppression that has differently impacted various groups of people. • Students learn about the history of racism, sexism, classism, homophobia, and religious intolerance, and how these forms of oppression have affected different communities. • Teachers make links between the historical roots of oppression and the impact it has on the experiences and material conditions of people today.	*Mamá the Alien/Mamá la Extraterrestre* by René Colato Laínez is a lighthearted story about a child who finds her mother's Resident Alien card and believes her to be an extraterrestrial. Video: *Small Truths: The Immigration Experience Through the Eyes of Children*. Explores immigration through children's perspectives. *Areli Is a Dreamer: A True Story* by Areli Morales recounts the author's life as an immigrant from Mexico and a DACA recipient (Dreamer).

Standards	Instruction
History/Social Science Content Standards (HSSCS) for CA 3.3.1: Research the explorers who visited here, the newcomers who settled here, and the people who continue to come to the region, including their cultural and religious traditions and contributions.	To introduce the concept of immigration, you might read aloud one of these texts, share your own family's immigration story or invite community members to share their own stories. Students can ask guest speakers questions to gather more information and clarify their understanding. Then, you might invite your students to reflect on the similarities and differences across stories.
HSSCS for CA 3.3.3: Trace why their community was established, how individuals and families contributed to its founding and development, and how the community has changed over time, drawing on maps, photographs, oral histories, letters, newspapers, and other primary sources.	Compare respectful representation of immigrants in *Dreamers* and/or *Carmela Full of Wishes* with less respectful books, such as *Chato's Kitchen* or *Skippyjon Jones*. Draw on historical community resources to identify how settlers and immigrants are portrayed. Discuss how respect for immigrants is or is not shown.
HSSCS for CA 3.3.3: Trace why their community was established, how individuals and families contributed to its founding and development, and how the community has changed over time, drawing on maps, photographs, oral histories, letters, newspapers, and other primary sources.	*Mamá the Alien/Mamá la Extraterrestre, Areli Is a Dreamer*, and the video, *Small Truths: The Immigration Experience Through the Eyes of Children*, are told from the perspective of children, helping students connect to and understand some of the oppression immigrants face. For example, students learn about why some people are considered "legal" but not others. Students can compare the experiences of the children in the book and video with their own lived experiences or those of their family and friends. No-cost, student-friendly material from sites like Learning for Justice or Newsela can spark discussions of what is legal and what is morally right.

Social Justice Element	Possible Texts
4. Social Movements and Social Change • Teachers share examples of movements of iconic and everyday people standing together to address the issues of social injustice they learned about in Element #3. • Teachers help students understand that by working together, people have united to create change.	Video: *Small Truths: The Immigration Experience Through the Eyes of Children* *Dolores Huerta: A Hero to Migrant Workers* by Sarah Warren *Side by Side/Lado a lado: The Story of Dolores Huerta and Cesar Chavez/La historia de Dolores Huerta y César Chávez* (2020) by Monica Brown. (a bilingual book)
5. Awareness Raising • Teachers provide opportunities for students to teach others about the issues they have learned about.	Students actively raise awareness about immigration through a poster-making campaign, peer teaching, a student newspaper, or other creative ways. They are given the opportunity to share their new knowledge.
6. Social Action • Teachers provide opportunities to take action on issues that affect students and their communities. • Students identify issues they feel passionate about and learn the skills of creating change firsthand.	Students might write letters to members of Congress sharing what they learned about immigration, stating their opinion, and/or including possible changes to legislation. This would be one way to address the persuasive writing standard. Alternately, students might organize an event or social action at their school, similar to *A Day Without Immigrants*.

Standards	Instruction
HSSCS for CA 3.4.6: Describe the lives of American heroes who took risks to secure our freedoms (e.g., Anne Hutchinson, Benjamin Franklin, Thomas Jefferson, Abraham Lincoln, Frederick Douglass, Harriet Tubman, Martin Luther King, Jr.).	The video, *Small Truths: The Immigration Experience Through the Eyes of Children*, can be used to show the situation of everyday people. Students learn about the historical work for migrant farmworkers' rights by reading about Dolores Huerta. *Side by Side/Lado a lado* is a bilingual book that addresses the collaborative work of Huerta and Chavez. Students can compare and contrast the issues immigrants faced in the 1960s and today.
HSSCS for CA 3.4.2: Discuss the importance of public virtue and the role of citizens, including how to participate in a classroom, in the community, and in civic life.	After studying a social movement linked to immigration, students help raise awareness of the issue in their community. Students can create and display posters around the school, share what they learned with other classes, or write a school newspaper on the topic of immigration.
HSSCS for CA 3.4.2: Discuss the importance of public virtue and the role of citizens, including how to participate in a classroom, in the community, and in civic life.	Finally, students are given the opportunity to take action against the issue of social justice identified in Element #3. For example, students engage in a social movement through a letter-writing campaign to members of Congress addressing issues related to immigration or child detention.

Tools to Try

This chapter's tools will support you to integrate diverse texts across the content areas. These tools will help you look at both the big and small of your planning. Planning a unit allows you to think about the long arc of your work and scaffold instruction to help students think more deeply about these topics. We also know that selecting diverse texts for math and science integration is not always easy; Tool 5.2 contains questions you can ask yourself to help in the process.

Tool 5.1 Social Justice Unit Planner and Continuum

This tool will help you identify and analyze texts when planning a social justice curriculum. It will help you identify where particular texts might fall along the continuum and support you in building a unit. It will also help you assess your plans and think through a unit's progression. Note that how you choose to use books can be more important than which books are used.

When planning a unit for social justice, remember that how you choose to use books can be more important than which books are used.

Tool 5.1 Social Justice Unit Planner and Continuum

Social Justice Element	Possible Texts	Standards	Instruction
1. Self-Love and Knowledge • Teachers provide opportunities for students to learn who they are and where they come from. • Students study different aspects of their identities and associated histories. • Negative stereotypes about student identities are deconstructed.			
2. Respect for Others • Teachers provide students with opportunities to share knowledge about their own cultural background with their classmates. • A climate of respect for diversity is created through students' learning to listen with kindness and empathy to the experiences of their peers. • Students deconstruct stereotypes about their peers' identities.			
3. Issues of Social Injustice • Teachers move from celebrating diversity to an exploration of how diversity can be experienced as oppression that has differently impacted various groups of people. • Students learn about the history of racism, sexism, classism, homophobia, and religious intolerance, and how these forms of oppression have affected different communities. • Teachers make links between the historical roots of oppression and the impact it has on experiences and material conditions of people today.			
4. Social Movements and Social Change • Teachers share examples of movements of iconic and everyday people standing together to address the issues of social injustice they learned about in Element #3. • Teachers help students understand that by working together, people have united to create change.			
5. Awareness Raising • Teachers provide opportunities for students to teach others about the issues they have learned about.			
6. Social Action • Teachers provide opportunities to take action on issues that affect students and their communities. • Students identify issues they feel passionate about and learn the skills of creating change firsthand.			

Adapted from Picower, B. (2012). Using their words: Six elements of social justice curriculum design for the elementary classroom. *International Journal of Multicultural Education, 14*(1), 1–17.

CHAPTER 5 | How Do I Use Diverse Texts Across the Content Areas?

Tool 5.2 Questions to Consider When Selecting Diverse Texts for Math and Science

Use this tool to think through text selection for your math and science units. The tool prompts you to consider the text's relevance to the subject and the students, diversity of perspective, potential tie-ins with social justice issues, and opportunities for students to demonstrate their understanding of the mathematical or scientific concept.

Looking Ahead

- **Chapter 6** tools help you and your students assess and reflect on progress.

- **Chapter 7** tools help you self-reflect on possible internal resistance and communicate with families and administrators.

Tool 5.2 Questions to Consider When Selecting Diverse Texts for Math and Science

Questions for Math Text Selections	Teacher Responses
• Does this text represent an idea or problem that connects to students' lives and is connected to mathematics? • Can this text be used to solve or highlight a social justice issue through mathematics? • What other text(s) could support the same mathematical concept and show different ways to think about or solve the problem? • What texts will students create to demonstrate their understanding of the mathematical concept?	

Questions for Science Text Selections	Teacher Responses
• Does this text illustrate a relevant science-focused issue? • Do the scientific perspectives represented in the texts include perspectives from a variety of communities and cultural backgrounds? • Will I be able to connect the scientific data in the text to the lives of all students in my classroom? • What texts will students create to demonstrate their understanding of the scientific concept?	

Adapted from Colwell, J. (2019). Selecting texts for disciplinary literacy instruction. *The Reading Teacher, 72*(5), 631–637.

Voices from the Field

Casey Cissna
instructional coach

"Diverse biographies about scientists, mathematicians, and historical figures expand students' awareness of the world and the opportunities that are possible for them."

Casey Cissna, a White former third-grade and K–5 STEAM teacher at Mountain View Whisman School District in Mountain View, California, has integrated diverse books across all content areas. Reflecting on her experiences, she said, "My third-grade students loved literature-based math lessons, and I could tell my students felt more excitement when completing word problems related to a text we had just read aloud. Social studies is another excellent opportunity to incorporate diverse texts in your classroom. I put up a big world map on the wall of our room, and highlight different areas of the world that our texts focus on. After we read each book, we add a small picture of these books on our world map. At the end of the year, we have a world map filled with literature from all around the world! I also have a section of the classroom devoted to diverse literature related to our social studies unit, so students can select books for silent reading as they like."

Casey shared some specific book titles she has used across the curriculum: "For social studies, I have many favorites depending on the unit we are studying. For example, I may use *The Case for Loving: The Fight for Interracial Marriage* by Selina Alko or *The Youngest Marcher: The Story of Audrey Faye Hendricks, a Young Civil Rights Activist* by Cynthia Levinson. Other books are *Harvesting Hope: The Story of Cesar Chavez* by Kathleen Krull and *Henry's Freedom Box: A True Story from the Underground Railroad* by Ellen Levine. And I can't forget one of my absolute favorites, *The Other Side* by Jacqueline Woodson. My students are always really impacted by her powerful work about segregation."

She continued, "For science and STEAM, I focus on two categories of diverse literature. The first category includes real-life stories of those who have contributed to science, spanning all ages, races, religions, and backgrounds. For example, *Hidden Figures* by Margot Lee Shetterly with Winifred Conkling, *Counting on Katherine: How Katherine Johnson Saved Apollo 13* by Helaine Becker, or *Rachel Carson and Her Book That Changed the World* by Laurie Lawlor. The second category of books I look for is a *mirror* for students: books containing a young person exploring science. For example, *Ada Twist, Scientist* by Andrea Beaty or *The Most Magnificent Thing* by Ashley Spires."

Casey noted that one of the biggest challenges in using diverse books across the curriculum is planning and finding time to integrate the books. To overcome this challenge, she recommends using backward design: "Teachers can think about their larger unit and which books fit best, then set aside deliberate time for these books, and make their use meaningful for the students." Casey recommends starting with biographies. She said, "Biographies hold a special place in my heart, because students love learning real stories and seeing real faces.… Diverse biographies about scientists, mathematicians, and historical figures expand students' awareness of the world and the opportunities that are possible for them. There are so many excellent, diverse biographical picture books coming out, and series such as I Am, Who Was?, and I Survived chapter books."

Voices from the Field

Marissa Kieffer
teacher

"We try to add in things where we have the leniency to do so."

Marissa Kieffer, a Latinx fourth-grade teacher in Mount Pleasant Elementary School District in San José, California, likes to supplement her curriculum with diverse texts because she feels it provides perspectives that are otherwise missing.

Marissa explained, "In Social Studies we bring in current event topics. This year I made a unit about segregation and how it has changed throughout schooling. The students then compared that to today. And so we try to add things in where we have the leniency to do so."

Marissa gave an example of how reading diverse texts helped students better understand historical primary sources. She said, "We read the Declaration of Independence, which is not a diverse text whatsoever. And the kids were so angry. One of the girls couldn't stop saying, 'Where are the women? Why are the women not included? Why are we not talking about them?' Another kid asked, 'Why are they saying that all men are created equal when they had enslaved people, and they were stealing the land from the Native peoples?'"

Marissa continued, "At one point we read something else that gave them an entry point to these ideas, and they were able to connect it to a primary source document. And so while it might seem to some people like we're just reading a picture book, those picture books, and those ideas, and those conversations, lead to even deeper conversations when we're reading something that is more complex."

> "Those picture books, and those ideas, and those conversations, lead to even deeper conversations when we're reading something that is more complex."

CHAPTER 6 | How Do I Navigate Tricky Student Responses?

How Do I Navigate Tricky Student Responses?

CHAPTER 6

Big Idea

Student responses to issues of diversity can be unpredictable, as students often are echoing what they hear in their families and communities. It can be challenging to know what to say when you witness bias or racism in your classroom. We have been there. I (Allison) was unsure how to react when, in my first year teaching, I had a Latinx student named Anya express racism toward a Black peer, Jamal. When Jamal came into my class to complete some work, there was an empty seat next to Anya, so I asked him to sit there. Normally very quiet, Anya started shaking her head "no." In a very out-of-character moment, she got up from her seat, walked up to me, and "whispered"—way too loudly—that she was not allowed to sit next to Black people because "they're bad people" and "they steal."

Not my best teaching moment, I replied, "That's ridiculous," and ordered Anya to sit down next to Jamal, who had overheard everything. "I'm sorry," I said briefly to Jamal. Not knowing what to do, I tried to go back to the lesson. Anya, feeling stuck between obeying her teacher and obeying her parents, started crying. I had unwittingly placed her in an impossible situation. At 7 years old, Anya was only restating what she had heard at home—she was not to blame. Still, her comment and her reluctance to sit next to Jamal were hurtful. Also only 7 years old, Jamal had just experienced racism by a peer. Sadly, this likely wasn't the first time and wouldn't be the last time. I apologized to Jamal again as he left. I had a lot of thinking to do.

We can develop classroom norms and provide students with the language and tools to have productive conversations about differences. These actions will help students become outspoken advocates rather than bystanders on issues of equity.

CHAPTER 6 | How Do I Navigate Tricky Student Responses?

Creating Common Understandings

One way to support communication among students is to create common understandings of key concepts. Teachers can set the stage for productive, meaningful conversations by clarifying key terms from the beginning and reminding students throughout. In this section, we share some key terms for which students should have a shared understanding. You may choose to include other terms, such as *race, religion, dis/ability, gender, social class, segregation, discrimination,* or *bias*. For each term below, we provide a child-friendly definition.

Diversity Vocabulary

Stereotype	a negative (not nice) image or idea that makes fun of a group of people	
Perspective	the way you see or feel about something that can be different from how another person sees it	
Empathy	the ability to feel what someone else is feeling because you care about them a lot	
Respect	a way of treating someone that shows you care about who they are, even if they are different from you or have different beliefs than you do	
Active Listening	the practice of showing your full attention to the person speaking and trying to understand what they are saying (rather than respond)	
Tokenism	the practice of putting someone different into a group so that it looks like you are including everyone, but they do not get the same attention as others	

Teachers set the stage for productive conversations by creating shared understandings of key vocabulary and concepts.

We like to use a Cognitive Content Dictionary, a Guided Language Acquisition Design™ (GLAD) strategy to teach vocabulary. This involves using a table like the one below. It is completed collaboratively with students over the course of a few days and serves as an anchor chart during class discussions to support students in using important terms consistently and accurately.

New Word	Students' Prediction	Definition	Used in a Sentence	
Perspective (n)	the way you see something	a point of view, often personal	Her *perspective* as a student was that the class had too much homework, but the teacher disagreed.	

CHAPTER 6 | How Do I Navigate Tricky Student Responses?

Setting Up for Success

Setting up classroom norms and practicing respectful language are critical steps for preparing students to engage in deep conversations about diverse topics. This section focuses on creating classroom expectations to prevent moments like the one with Anya.

Classroom Norms

First and foremost, you'll want to co-develop classroom norms that address how students interact with one another during discussions. These can be interactively co-written and posted in a highly visible place in the classroom. Norms might include: respecting all perspectives, active listening, always using respectful language, helping one another communicate effectively, and asking for clarification. Reviewing the norms frequently and holding students accountable to them are important parts of ensuring respectful conversations. Below we share the norms we have used in our classrooms, and invite you to make them your own or create your own. A student-friendly version of the norms follows.

- **Respect all perspectives.** Developmentally, young children are consumed by their own needs and desires, and they struggle to understand the perspectives of others. Respect for others' perspectives, even if students are too young to *understand* those perspectives, is a starting point.

- **Listen to understand.** Active listening involves listening to understand rather than listening to respond. Listening to understand helps students begin to comprehend others' voices and experiences. It requires students to withhold judgment, self-monitor their understanding, and ask clarifying questions aimed at better understanding others' voices and experiences. Listening to understand is an ongoing journey.

- **Always use respectful language.** Consistency of respectful language is the foundation for trust in your classroom. Therefore, use of respectful language is nonnegotiable—no exceptions. Students should feel safe, knowing there is no threat of being called a negative word based on their race, class, dis/ability, gender, etc. In this section, we share tools and strategies to help students develop respectful language, as well as some strategies for what to do in the case of mishaps.

- **Help one another communicate effectively.** Talking about race, religion, dis/ability, and other sensitive issues can be difficult at any age. Ask students to commit to help one another during these conversations. This creates a collaborative spirit and eases the responsibility on the individual, who knows they can ask for the correct term if it isn't coming to mind immediately. It also opens the door for students to kindly correct one another and be open to that correction. Talking about differences, although challenging, enables students to provide and accept support from one another.

- **Ask for clarification.** Communication between people—getting ideas from one person's head into words so that another person can understand—is always challenging.

Misunderstandings can occur when one person does not understand the intent or meaning of another person's communication. Misunderstandings can also occur when there are good intentions and the speaker, knowingly or unknowingly, communicates deficit beliefs about people and communities.

To reduce misunderstandings, ask students to reserve judgment and ask clarifying questions to make sure they understand the other person's point of view. On the following page, we provide some examples of clarifying questions.

> **Read this!**
>
> Kay, M. R. (2018). *Not light, but fire: How to lead meaningful race conversations in the classroom.* Stenhouse Publishers. This book details how to facilitate powerful discussions about difficult topics and shares useful student conversations as examples.

Sample Clarifying Questions

- Let me check to see if I understand. Did you mean _____?
- Can you please say that in a different way? I'm not sure I understood.
- Can you give an example to help me understand?

Sample Anchor Chart of Norms with Kid-Friendly Language

Classroom Norms

Respect all perspectives.
People are different; we value and respect differences.

Listen to understand.
We listen actively, think about what we understand, and ask questions if we aren't sure.

Always use respectful language.
Every human deserves respect.

Help one another communicate effectively.
We help each other talk about differences respectfully.

Ask for clarification.
We ask clarifying questions to better understand another's point of view.

Consistently reviewing the norms and providing examples of when they are being followed will help students internalize the classroom expectations.

Sticky Notes and Prompts

Developmentally, young children struggle to understand the perspectives of others. Intentionally practicing perspective-taking through read-alouds, writing prompts, and other literacy acts can help students become more empathetic toward their peers. Specifically, students will develop an understanding of how their actions and words can impact others. Next are some strategies to prepare students for these conversations.

> "Intentionally practicing perspective-taking through read-alouds, writing prompts, and other literacy acts can help students become more empathetic toward their peers."

Sticky Note Reminders

When you are having trouble remembering to use a new term, or if you are trying to stay focused on a key idea, sticky note reminders are a helpful tool. By using sticky notes, you model part of the learning process and normalize it for students. You can show students how to use sticky note reminders as a learning tool as they practice using new terms or discussion prompts.

Prompts and Prompting Cards

Since talking about diverse topics is hard for adults, we can't assume it will be any easier for children. You can help students by providing discussion prompts and/or language for them to use during conversations. Prompts may be presented on anchor charts or prompting cards for individual students, and/or provided orally when you observe that a student needs support. On the following page are some examples of prompts we have used.

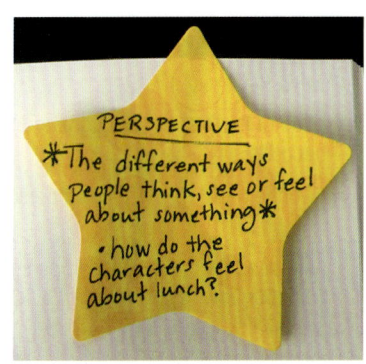

Sticky notes can help students (and teachers) remember to use new terms or discussion prompts.

CHAPTER 6 | How Do I Navigate Tricky Student Responses?

Discussion Prompting Cards

Connections

Grades K–2

- This book reminds me of _____ [insert text-to-self connection].
- This book makes me feel _____.

Grades 3–5

- This text reminds me of _____ [current or historical event] because _____.
- I can connect this text to my community because _____.
- If I were _____ [character name], I would feel _____ when _____.

Reaching Understanding

Grades K–2

- It isn't fair that _____. Why did that happen?
- Why does _____ [insert person/character] look _____ [insert emotion] in the picture?

Grades 3–5

- What did _____ [insert person/character] mean when they said _____?
- I did not understand when/why _____. Can you help me understand?

Texts as Mirrors

Grades K–2

- I saw myself/my family/my community in this book when _____.
- This book makes me feel good about myself because _____.
- I think my mom/dad/grandma/aunt would like this book because _____.

Grades 3–5

- I connected with _____ character in the book because _____.
- This text makes me feel proud of _____ because _____.

Texts as Windows and Doors

Grades K–2

- I did not connect to this book. Some important differences between the book and me are _____.
- This book helped me understand _____.

Grades 3–5

- I did not connect to this text because _____.
- I would like to offer another interpretation from a different perspective. _____.

Criticality Lens

Grades K–2

- I do not think my mom/dad/grandma/aunt would like this book because _____.
- I wonder how _____ [insert person/character] feels about _____.
- I noticed that _____ [insert person/character] tells the story. I wonder how the book would be different if _____ [insert person/character] told it. I think _____.

Criticality Lens

Grades 3–5

- I noticed that the voice(s) of _____ was/were missing from this text.
- I noticed that this story was told from just one perspective, the perspective of _____. Another perspective to consider might be _____.
- The illustrations in this book treat character differences respectfully/disrespectfully. For example, on page _____ the illustration _____.
- I did not appreciate this book. I think the book promotes stereotypes by _____.

For a reproducible version of the prompting cards, see Tool 6.1 on page 167.

Self-Reflection

Self-reflection in the context of learning to have productive conversations about diversity can take many forms. Self-reflection should become a habit. Below we share some instructional supports to help students develop this habit:

- You may choose to have students reflect upon their participation in the discussion or their progress toward enacting one or more norms.

- Co-developing a discussion rubric from the norms can help students locate where they are in the progression and help them identify next steps.

- Students can reflect on their use of discussion prompts.

You might also choose to have consistent reflection questions that students answer, either orally or in writing, after each discussion. Questions should be kept to a minimum and might focus on the amount and quality of the student's participation as well as next steps. On the following page are some examples.

> **Quick Tip**
>
> Remember that not all students will connect to all texts, and acknowledging that is the first step to questioning why and considering the book's perspective.

A co-developed discussion rubric can support student self-reflection on their participation and progress.

CHAPTER 6 | How Do I Navigate Tricky Student Responses?

Grades K–2: Self-reflection in the primary grades is guided by the teacher. It might include students talking to a partner or using icons such as variations of a smiley face to self-reflect. Be explicit about when students might circle the smiley face—for example, when they did not hurt anyone else's feelings. Possible post-discussion self-reflection questions may include:

1. How was my participation in today's discussion?
2. What can I do differently tomorrow?
   - listen more carefully
   - stay on topic
   - connect to other students' comments
   - ask another student a question
   - invite another student into the conversation
   - participate more
   - participate less so that others can participate more

For a reproducible version of the self-reflection questions, see Tool 6.2 on page 169.

> "Once self-reflection becomes a habit, it leads to self-awareness and the ability to recognize how our actions and language affect others."

Grades 3 and Up: In third grade and up, students can self-reflect more independently. You might choose to collect these reflections daily as exit tickets or have students write in a journal that they review every few weeks. Possible self-reflection questions may include:

1. How was my participation in today's discussion?
   - Amount – Did I talk too much? Too little? Did I intentionally include others in the discussion?
   - Respect – Was my language respectful throughout the conversation?
   - Quality – Did I move the conversation forward by challenging any ideas or identifying missing/other perspectives?
2. What could I have done differently or better?
3. How will I remember to do that next time?

Once self-reflection becomes a habit, it leads to self-awareness and the ability to recognize how our actions and language affect others. We created Tool 6.2, Student Self-Reflection Questions, as a starting place for you.

Older students can self-reflect more independently using daily exit tickets or a journal that you review periodically with them.

CHAPTER 6 | How Do I Navigate Tricky Student Responses?

Beginning the Conversations

Small-group discussion enables students to practice being both equitable contributors and active listeners.

Following the suggestions described in this chapter will set your students up to have productive dialogue by focusing on the *how*. As teachers, we can often focus on the *what*—what students learn (the content)—and neglect the *how*—how they talk about it. So this work is critical. However, once terms are defined, norms are established, and prompts have been practiced, it is time to bring them all together in authentic conversations about diversity. Start slowly and focus on concrete goals. Get students talking and listening, and be available to model how to do this work in real time.

As these conversations occur more frequently and for longer durations, there will inevitably be more times when you are not around to name and address problematic comments. This is a good development! However, this means students will need some tools to advocate for themselves, or others, in your absence. We have found the Ouch Option, or Empathy Stop, to be an effective way for children to express their discomfort and be heard.

> "As teachers, we can often focus on the *what*—what students learn (the content)—and neglect the *how*—how they talk about it."

Small-Group Practice

The next step is to explicitly practice conversations about difficult topics and scaffold student talk. This can start in a whole-group setting, but it is important that students have practice in small groups as well, whether or not you are immediately present. The end goal is always student independence. Visit with each of the groups to hear their ideas, provide feedback, and assess. You can initially limit, and then slowly expand, the amount of time students discuss in small groups before calling them back together. Back in the whole-group setting, tricky pieces of small-group conversations can be shared, along with explicit strategies for working through the issues raised. The short segments of time and explicit conversations about how to have respectful conversations will support students' independence in the future.

> **Quick Tip**
>
> A fishbowl discussion has a smaller, inner circle that participates in the discussion while a larger, outer circle listens carefully to the ideas presented. Students take turns in these roles so that they practice being both contributors and listeners. This strategy is especially useful when you want to make sure all students participate in a discussion.

The Ouch Option or Empathy Stop Strategy

Sometimes, a student might inadvertently hurt another student's feelings. The Ouch Option allows students to identify when this happens so that the feelings can be addressed and do not resurface later in negative ways. For example, if one student says something that accidentally hurts another student's feelings, the second student can say "ouch" and immediately address why their feelings were hurt by what was said. If you are an upper-grade teacher, you may prefer to ask students to say "empathy stop" instead of "ouch." This allows them to attach vocabulary that is developmentally appropriate, but if "ouch" gets the job done, that is fine, too. The larger goal is to open dialogue and support students in understanding how their words impact others.

CHAPTER 6 | How Do I Navigate Tricky Student Responses?

The Ouch Option, or Empathy Stop, is best taught in a whole-group setting, such as a fishbowl demonstration, and practiced in small groups, where the affective filter may be lower. Students employ an Empathy Stop when they notice that something said by one student is experienced by another student as a *microaggression* (meaning that it upsets another student for any reason). When a microaggression occurs, any student has the opportunity and responsibility to say, "ouch," or "empathy stop," and shift the conversation to why the comment might be hurtful. Let's look at an example of a conversation below where a teacher uses this strategy when a White student and an Asian student surface a common stereotype:

Sami: Michael said all Asians are smart. Is that true?

Awesome Teacher: That's a great question, Sami. Friends, what do you think? Do you think all people in a group are any one thing? For instance, are all girls nice? Or mean?

Students: No. Some are nice. But others are mean!

Awesome Teacher: That's right, remember our vocabulary word, *stereotype*? When we say that *all* people in a group are one way it's usually a stereotype. Let's look at our word wall for a definition. A stereotype is a negative (not nice) image or idea that makes fun of a group of people.

Sami: But Awesome Teacher, being called smart isn't negative. It's good to be smart.

Awesome Teacher: You're often right, Sami, but in this case, it's still a stereotype because it says *everyone* in a group is a particular way, and because it's often used to make fun instead of being used in a nice way. This is a great example of a time when you might want to use an Empathy Stop, Sami. You were uncomfortable with something that Michael said, so you have every right to stop the conversation there and get clarification. How does that sound for next time?

Interrupting comments about stereotypes and other misconceptions students have about differences is helpful. Addressing these issues immediately, like Awesome Teacher did, is helpful because it usually prevents them from festering—often on the playground. However, it's also fine to take time to think through how you want to address an issue. Reading a book about the topic with the class can help bring the discussion back in focus and squash misconceptions.

Using time to explicitly practice having conversations about differences in the short term can have significant payoffs in the long term, as it enables students to have productive conversations without the teacher present. It can also reduce fears some teachers may have about allowing students to work in small groups, such as book clubs or literature circles, when the topic is one of diversity.

Quick Tip

Selecting the right text to expose and subsequently respond to difficult topics is key. Use what you have learned about your students to find content that will uncover blind spots in their thinking or open a path for marginalized students to share their experiences.

An Important Note About This Strategy

It is important to shift the responsibility for Empathy Stops from people of color and marginalized groups to others. We do not want to put the onus on marginalized people—and especially children of color—to defend against stereotypes. It is important to ensure that everyone has the opportunity to use Empathy Stops if they would like. However, all group members should be thinking about how language will be perceived by others—both those who are present and those who are not.

CHAPTER 6 | How Do I Navigate Tricky Student Responses?

> **Read this!**
>
> Hagerman, M. A. (2019). Conversations with kids about race. *Phi Delta Kappan, 100*(7), 17–21. This article explains that students are already having conversations about race and similar topics. It asks: Wouldn't you rather know what students are saying and help them navigate those topics?

Observational Notes as Formative Assessment

While particular student comments might stand out to us as especially effective or troublesome, it is difficult to remember exactly what students say when there are so many students and so much happening during the day. Observational notes taken during classroom discussions can help you identify who spoke, how frequently, and can even help you gauge the relevance or quality of each student's comments.

Observational notes can also help you identify the next instructional steps with particular students. In the Appendix you will find an Observation Tool for Discussions About Diversity that can help you identify what to look for during classroom discussions. The tool is currently set up for small-group observation, with spaces for only six students at the top, but it can also be adapted for use in whole-class settings.

Observational notes taken during whole-class or small-group discussions can help you gauge the amount, relevance, and quality of individual students' comments as well as identify instructional next steps.

When Challenges Persist

Sometimes, despite having set up classroom norms and done all of the above, there may still be difficult moments when students' reactions to issues of diversity challenge you. Here we provide a few suggestions for handling tricky student responses.

Rephrasing Student Responses
Explicitly rephrasing student responses in more respectful ways can help students learn to use language in more mature ways. For example, a student might refer to a character in a book as "that handicapped character" or "that kid in a wheelchair." In response, you can acknowledge the student's idea and rephrase it using the more appropriate "child with a dis/ability," and explain that we put the person before the dis/ability.

Asking Other Students to Rephrase
Similar to rephrasing, you may ask other students to rephrase. Using the above example, you might say, "Yes, the idea is good. Who can help us rephrase that statement in a more respectful way that puts the person before the dis/ability?" In this way, students are helping one another acquire respectful language.

> "Sometimes, despite having set up classroom norms ... there may still be difficult moments when students' reactions to issues of diversity challenge you."

Quick Correction and Follow-Up Discussion

In the very rare cases in which a student might have used inappropriate language intentionally, it is best to quickly correct the student's language use and have a one-on-one follow-up conversation as soon as possible. That conversation would include probing to determine if the student understands the meaning of the inappropriate word and whether they intended to use it in a hurtful manner. The conversation should also include a brief explanation of why we don't use such language, and examples of language that could be used instead. Of course, there are certain words that we simply cannot allow in the classroom.

Remember Not to Judge

At the end of the day, we have to remember that—except in rare cases of intentional use of abusive or inappropriate language—it is not the child's fault. And it is not our job to judge students' families. We, Allison and Claudia, have used inappropriate language ourselves and we have plenty of people in our families who use inappropriate language when talking about differences in groups, so we do not want to throw stones while living in glass houses. As educators, our job is to educate our students about differences to help them think critically about labels and language use, and to provide alternative, respectful language for them to use in school.

> "If we teach our students, from an early age, to speak against language that belittles and hurts others, we have a better chance of building the next generation of advocates."

Teaching Students to Speak Up

As we all know from personal experience, it can be difficult for children (and adults) to stand up to others when they hear disrespectful or hurtful language around race, ability, gender, sexuality, or any other difference. If we teach our students, from an early age, to speak against language that belittles and hurts others, we have a better chance of building the next generation of advocates. A student does not need to be gay or Black to stand up to homophobia or racism. The more advocates for justice that we can develop in our classrooms, the more likely the next generation will be more accepting.

For this reason, it is important that we teach students to talk about issues of diversity respectfully, and also to speak up against biased, discriminatory, or derogatory comments of any kind. We want to develop a sense of unity, where students stick up for one another. This takes the onus off the minoritized group. The Muslim student, the student with a dis/ability, and the transgender student learn to advocate for themselves, and for one another. They also know that others will speak up on their behalf. With this sense of unity come love and respect for difference. Building the skills to talk about diversity and love for others can happen early, when children are still young.

This work is challenging and requires courage to stand against prejudice and discrimination, even when you are not exactly sure what to say or how to say it. We have often heard teachers say that they did not initiate challenging conversations in their classrooms because they did not know what to say and did not want to say the wrong thing. However, by remaining silent you are communicating, at the very least, that the conversation is not worth having. Your silence may also communicate agreement that your students pick up on. We encourage you to speak up and accept that you will make missteps in this work. We all do. The important thing is to model to your students that you are willing to put in the work, and that you will correct your mistakes and do better each time.

Tools to Try

This chapter's tools are intended to support students' talk about diverse texts. Tool 6.1 can help get students talking about diverse books by providing language to scaffold whole- and small-group discussions. The purpose is to give students language that they can hold on to while they build their expertise in talking about diverse topics. After some practice, you and your students will want to check in on progress. Students can self-reflect using Tool 6.2.

Tool 6.1 Discussion Prompting Cards

The Discussion Prompting Cards support discussion by providing language for students to use. Six cards provide prompts for students in grades K–2 and 3–5 to address Connections, Reaching Understanding, Texts as Mirrors, Texts as Windows and Doors, and Criticality Lens. Students will likely have a lot to say; the prompts are just a starting place to get the conversation going.

Despite your best preparations, mishaps in communication may still occur. What is important is that you model the willingness to put in the work and correct your mistakes going forward.

Tool 6.1 Discussion Prompting Cards

Connections

Grades K–2

- This book reminds me of _____ [insert text-to-self connection].
- This book makes me feel _____.

Grades 3–5

- This text reminds me of _____ [current or historical event] because _____.
- I can connect this text to my community because _____.
- If I were _____ [character name], I would feel _____ when _____.

Reaching Understanding

Grades K–2

- It isn't fair that _____. Why did that happen?
- Why does _____ [insert person/character] look _____ [insert emotion] in the picture?

Grades 3–5

- What did _____ [insert person/character] mean when they said _____?
- I did not understand when/why _____. Can you help me understand?

Texts as Mirrors

Grades K–2

- I saw myself/my family/my community in this book when _____.
- This book makes me feel good about myself because _____.
- I think my mom/dad/grandma/aunt would like this book because _____.

Grades 3–5

- I connected with _____ character in the book because _____.
- This text makes me feel proud of _____ because _____.

Texts as Windows and Doors

Grades K–2

- I did not connect to this book. Some important differences between the book and me are _____.
- This book helped me understand _____.

Grades 3–5

- I did not connect to this text because _____.
- I would like to offer another interpretation from a different perspective. _____.

Criticality Lens

Grades K–2

- I do not think my mom/dad/grandma/aunt would like this book because _____.
- I wonder how _____ [insert person/character] feels about _____.
- I noticed that _____ [insert person/character] tells the story. I wonder how the book would be different if _____ [insert person/character] told it. I think _____.

Criticality Lens

Grades 3–5

- I noticed that the voice(s) of _____ was/were missing from this text.
- I noticed that this story was told from just one perspective, the perspective of _____. Another perspective to consider might be _____.
- The illustrations in this book treat character differences respectfully/disrespectfully. For example, on page _____ the illustration _____.
- I did not appreciate this book. I think the book promotes stereotypes by _____.

CHAPTER 6 | How Do I Navigate Tricky Student Responses?

Tool 6.2 Student Self-Reflection Questions

Use these questions to help students self-reflect after discussion. The consistent use of a few key questions will help students develop self-reflection as a habit.

Variations are provided for students in grades K–2 and 3–5. Younger students can have questions read to them and circle answers, or they can read and circle answers for themselves. Self-reflection is the key to self-awareness, which helps students recognize how their language and actions affect others.

Looking Ahead

- **Chapter 7** tools help you self-reflect on possible internal resistance and communicate with families and administrators.

Student self-reflection fosters self-awareness, which helps students recognize how their language and actions affect others.

168

Tool 6.2 Student Self-Reflection Questions

Grades K–2:

Name: _____

1. How was my participation in today's discussion?

2. What can I do differently tomorrow? (Tell a partner or write one sentence.)

- listen more carefully

- stay on topic

- connect to other students' comments

- ask another student a question

- invite another student into the conversation

- participate more

- participate less so that others can participate more

Grades 3 and Up:

1. How was my participation in today's discussion?

- **Amount** – Did I talk too much? Too little? Did I intentionally include others in the discussion?

- **Respect** – Was my language respectful throughout the conversation?

- **Quality** – Did I move the conversation forward by challenging any ideas or identifying missing/other perspectives?

2. What could I have done differently or better?

3. How will I remember to do that next time?

Voices from the Field

Michelle Rosas-Gonzalez
teacher

"It is important for teachers to know common misconceptions that may exist within the communities they work with."

Michelle Rosas-Gonzalez is a bilingual fourth-grade elementary school teacher in Sunnyvale School District in Sunnyvale, California. Michelle identifies as Xicana and is in her fifth year of teaching. Michelle begins by setting up classroom norms. She works on "giving students that freedom, that agency to come up with their own norms." She adds, "You can group the norms, and make sure to include or address any that are essential or may not have been addressed." To allow for anonymity, Michelle uses sticky notes to collect responses from students. Once the class has developed their norms, Michelle posts them where they are visible and students can return to them throughout the year.

Michelle recognizes that it is important to support students' use of respectful language; however, she explains that the work begins with teachers. She says, "First of all, it's important that we as educators know the language. So, before you go out there and hold the student accountable, you yourself have to know it. You have to be ready, especially just grappling with all the *isms*. If you're talking about ableism, or the LGBTQ+ community, you have to come prepared."

She also believes it is important for teachers to know common misconceptions that may exist within the communities they work with and be ready to correct them. Michelle explained, "It's helpful to know the misconceptions that may already exist, depending on the community. Since I've worked with an incredibly diverse group of students, predominantly Latin bilingual people, I already kind of had an idea of possible misconceptions around autism. I remember one of my students said, 'O es que está malito, está enfermito' (Oh, it means that he is unwell; he is sick)."

She continued, "You want to be careful about a few things, like your tone of voice. You don't say, 'Oh, no, no, they're not *malitos*! Why would you say that!?' Instead, you might say, 'Oh, that's interesting that you say that.' It's okay to address it. Something like, 'Friends, actually, that's not true.' It's okay to call it out, but be careful with your tone of voice. 'That's not true, friends. Autism has to do more with the way that certain friends develop in their brains. *No están malitos* (They are not unwell/ill). There's nothing wrong with them. They just happen to think in a different way. And they happen to develop a little bit differently.' So, definitely don't strike any student down. Don't reprimand them. Just address it in a way that's respectful."

When we asked Michelle how the student and the class responded, she said, "I think the student felt a little bit bad. Like, 'Oh, I didn't mean it like that.' And that's where the Safe Space comes in. I assured the student, 'It's okay if you thought that before.' Once you address it, students understand. You reinforce it by using that same language. You always come back to it and find different ways to reinforce those crucial ideas."

Michelle encourages teachers to make it a practice to select "diverse texts where… the characters are relatively diverse and they engage in some kind of joyful activity or something that has nothing to do with potential problems their community might encounter. While you may want to address problems that exist within those communities, you also want to normalize their humanity… because that is our goal as teachers."

Voices from the Field

Marissa Kieffer
teacher

"I had to explain, [one person] doesn't speak for the whole community.... We have to have those conversations."

Marissa Kieffer is a Latinx fourth-grade teacher in Mount Pleasant Elementary School District in San José, California. She chooses to supplement the school's Language Arts curriculum to include more diversity.

Unfortunately, the N-word is included in a fourth-grade curricular text. She explained, "They have included the usage of the N-word in the text. So we have a conversation about why we're not going to use that word, what we're going to use instead, and why that word is hurtful. They also use 'slaves' instead of 'enslaved people.' So we address and change those words along the way. When we had that conversation, one student in our class said, 'I can use the N-word because he [a Black student] said it was okay.' And I had to explain, [one person] doesn't speak for the whole community. He can't just give someone a free pass to use a word that causes pain. We have to have those conversations."

Marissa's students learn to kindly challenge one another's ideas, so it usually does not fall on her to do so. She explained, "The class was discussing *Love Is Love*, which is about gay parents and diverse families. A student commented, 'That's not okay. They can't get married.' Another child responded, 'Wait, my cousin just got married to another guy. And it was fine.' Having [shared community norms] established helps the conversation continue in a positive way. But there are definitely preconceived notions that come into the classroom."

Marissa shared that on occasion, students' families have disagreed with her approach. She explained that one parent was upset when they read an article about the events of January 6, 2021. She said, "The kids were talking about what they saw on the news and how they felt about it. One parent was very upset and told me I didn't have the right to talk to her child about the incident. The parent thought it should be handled as a family discussion and believed that her daughter didn't know anything about the day's event. But her daughter was the most knowledgeable student in our conversation. I explained to her that I used a district-adopted curriculum. And I told her, 'Your daughter had the most to say. She was very thoughtful, and she facilitated a lot of the conversation that was going on with other students.'"

Marissa also explained that she sometimes uses diverse texts in response to students' comments. She said that she plans a lot of read-alouds, but also uses diverse texts in response to classroom observations. For example, she explained that she might choose a particular book "if a student makes a comment or there's some kind of breakdown in the class. For example, one day we were having a conversation and someone said, 'Oh, that's so gay.' So we talked about it in the moment, and after recess we did a read-aloud and discussed how families look different ways." Marissa uses the texts both proactively across the curriculum, and also reactively, based on what's going on with her students.

CHAPTER 7 | I Still Have Concerns, How Do I Move Forward?

I Still Have Concerns, How Do I Move Forward?

CHAPTER 7

Big Idea

T he previous chapters have explored why teachers should use diverse books, including some of the relevant theory and research; what to look for when selecting diverse books; and ways to use them in language arts classes and across the curriculum. This chapter is where the hard work happens—the internal work that helps us identify and conquer our own biases and internal resistance. This is difficult and often uncomfortable. We urge you to embrace the discomfort as an important part of the process. It doesn't always feel good, but the results—the impact on our kids—is worth it. We invite you into, or deeper into, this work with us.

As Kendi (2019) tells us, there is an important distinction between not being actively racist and being anti-racist. This is the difference between not spreading hate and actively working against that hate. You can avoid spreading hate but still be complicit in racism by remaining silent as you witness and do nothing to interfere in the suffering inflicted by racism. We argue that the same is true for other aspects of diversity, such as dis/ability, gender identity, sexual orientation, religion, etc. While not addressing them in your classroom may be less harmful than you being explicitly ableist, sexist, or homophobic in your teaching, when your students do not see themselves reflected in your curriculum and instruction, it can still have negative effects.

Our internal fears can derail our efforts to become the kind of teacher we aspire to be. Teaching from a place of love and openness, rather than from fear, enables us to move forward as educators for justice. This work is hard and we encourage you to do it anyway.

CHAPTER 7 | I Still Have Concerns, How Do I Move Forward?

They're Not Too Young

Teachers can help children learn how to respect and talk about differences in positive ways.

Society has conditioned us to ignore skin and color differences among people. It can be deemed impolite to notice or bring up personal differences in conversation. But children notice differences. Unless we help them learn how to respect and talk about differences, they find their own way—and playground talk is often not respectful.

Assuming the primary grades are too early to start talking about race and other human differences, teachers often ask us at what grade they should begin addressing these topics and using diverse books. We try to help them see the privilege behind that question. Parents of students with dis/abilities and BIPOC parents (among others) often do not have the option to delay those conversations. In contrast, some White parents—and even some parents of color—wanting to protect their children from issues of race, try to avoid conversations with their children about it. Kids will talk about race regardless of parents' preferences, so providing them with the tools to do so can only be helpful (Hagerman, 2019).

> "Unless we help them learn how to respect and talk about differences, they find their own way—and playground talk is often not respectful."

In our experience, internal resistance and fear are the primary reasons teachers tend not to address issues of diversity in the classroom. In this chapter, we consider how to address our own internal resistance. As Kendi (2019) and others remind us, all humans have internal, possibly unconscious, biases. This was helpful from an evolutionary perspective: Knowing and being able to determine in-group from out-group was critical to survival in early humans. At the current stage of human evolution, however, it is important that we uncover our unconscious biases so that we can work to overcome them. This is very personal and difficult work, and we encourage you to treat yourself with love and compassion as you challenge yourself on your personal journey. We do not mean that you stop the work or stop fully examining the harm your instructional choices may have caused in the past because it is too hard. Instead, we ask you to reflect, learn, and look for ways to improve how you integrate diverse social and historical perspectives into your curriculum.

For example, in my (Allison's) first year of teaching, I was planning to ignore Black History Month. The superficial reasons for ignoring it were plenty: State testing was just around the corner, I was behind in the district's pacing guide, there was nothing related to Black history in our Language Arts curriculum, and I did not have any Black students in my class. However, the truth is that I was uncomfortable with the topic and felt completely unprepared to teach it.

Two things happened that impacted my thinking. First, a Latinx student, Anya, expressed anti-Black sentiments (explained in Chapter 6). Second, our Black librarian, Yselda, asked me what I was planning to do for Black History Month. That year, with Yselda's help, I made a highly imperfect attempt. But I acknowledged my missteps, moved through regrets, learned more, and reasserted my commitment to do better for all my students. The work is too important to stop just because it made me uncomfortable.

CHAPTER 7 | I Still Have Concerns, How Do I Move Forward?

Conquering Our Internal Resistance

Internal resistance is powerful and can result in rationalizing reasons for not using diverse texts with students. There are as many reasons for internal resistance as there are teachers. You can assess your own internal resistance using Tool 7.1, Where Is My Resistance Coming From? Self-reflection is critical for anti-racist and inclusive teaching.

Working with hundreds of teachers has led us to identify five common concerns that teachers have about using diverse texts and addressing controversial topics in their classrooms. These concerns include:

1. Feeling that they are not knowledgeable enough about a culture or issue to "teach" it.
2. Fear of other adults' perceptions of their use of diverse texts, primarily parents and administrators.
3. Concern about students' reactions to the lesson or book.
4. Not being personally comfortable with the topic themselves.
5. Concern that other people will think it self-centered to teach a topic that directly relates to them.

Next, we address each of these very valid concerns individually.

> "Internal resistance is powerful and can result in rationalizing reasons for not using diverse texts with students."

1. **"I'm not knowledgeable enough about this topic to teach it. What if I say something wrong?"**

Problem: In this instance, you want to include a book about a diverse topic, but you feel you do not have enough background knowledge about the topic to do it justice. You might be concerned about using the wrong terms and possibly offending someone.

Possible Solutions: First, show yourself some love for acknowledging your own lack of knowledge about a topic. You're right—schools of the past did not do justice to perspectives or histories other than the dominant mainstream story. Next, develop a quick plan to become just a little bit more knowledgeable, and then a little more, and then a little more. And, remember that you do not need to have a doctoral degree about a topic before you can read a book about it to your students.

A quick Internet search will likely help you get an overview of the topic, but you'll still want to dig deeper. Look for more recent resources to determine the appropriate terms (e.g., Black or African American? Gay or queer?), as language changes over time. Podcasts, interviews, videos, audiobooks, and traditional or e-books are all good resources. Multiple books have also been written to address exactly this problem. Some of the best known are Howard Zinn's (2015) *A People's History of the United States* and James W. Loewen's (2007) *Lies My Teacher Told Me: Everything Your American History Textbook Got Wrong*. Roxanne Dunbar-Ortiz (2014) authored *An Indigenous Peoples' History of the United States*, and Michael Bronski (2011) wrote *A Queer History of the United States*. These are just a few examples. The problem is systemic and societal. You are part of the solution.

Finally, do not be afraid to admit what you do not know. Tell your students that you are also learning about the topic, and motivate them to learn along with you. You can even tell them that you are working on using appropriate language.

CHAPTER 7 | I Still Have Concerns, How Do I Move Forward?

> **Quick Tip**
>
> If you do not feel safe discussing certain topics because you are still processing, recovering, or healing your own marginalized identities, honor your needs and your individual process. As you heal, take some time to learn about people and topics that make you uncomfortable because you know little about them. You are an important part of this work.

Talk to parents, community members, and friends about it. In most cases, they are thrilled to be invited to share their experiences and knowledge with students. Let them know that you are still learning and would appreciate their expertise. If you are able, show them that you value their time and expertise by writing a thoughtful letter or treating them to coffee or dessert. Finally, treat yourself with compassion as you learn. Remind yourself that learning is a process and to enjoy the journey. No one can know everything—not even teachers!

2. **"What will my students' parents or my school principal say if I use this book about _____? I don't want to be considered a troublemaker."**

Problem: Teachers tend to be rule followers, which is often a good thing. However, it can mean that those who do things a little differently may be considered troublemakers by their administrators or peers. We have seen this concern most often with LGBTQ+ issues. When we act based on a fear of what others *might* think, we unnecessarily cede our agency and allow others to control the curriculum. While it is a valid and understandable fear, overcoming it is important to more confidently share diverse books with children.

This problem can be different for teachers from marginalized communities. The reactions and consequences could be worse for a gay teacher teaching about gender identity or a Black teacher teaching about anti-Black racism. A gay teacher discussing gender identity or homosexuality could be perceived as promoting an agenda simply by having these conversations. A Black teacher discussing anti-Black racism could be accused of being angry or aggressive, and be chastised for making everything about race.

Possible Solutions: If this is a real concern for you, let people know in advance that you will be using a book in your class that addresses a particular topic. Because you know how to select and analyze children's books (from Chapter 3), any books you select will deal with issues of diversity in appropriate and respectful ways. A quick email to families/caregivers that briefly explains your reasoning, and an invitation to have parents preview the book or talk about questions or concerns, will usually suffice. If people have concerns, they will let you know. More often than not, showing the concerned parent or administrator the book will ease their fears. For example, in *Call Me Max* (2019), the main character is a transgender kindergarten student. See a sample email below to parents from a third-grade teacher. (Guidelines for writing these types of emails can be found in Tool 7.2.)

> Dear Families of Room 22,
>
> Due to some recent student comments about gender norms, next week in class we will be reading the book *Call Me Max* (2019) by Kyle Lukoff. As always, please feel free to reach out if you have any questions, or if you would like to preview the book before we read it on Tuesday. The main character is a transgender kindergarten student who experiences some bullying and other difficulties as he transitions from home to kindergarten. As always in room 22, the expectation is that all people will be treated with respect and dignity. This book gives us the opportunity to address gender norms explicitly to ensure that we treat one another with respect while addressing our grade-level standards. Students will describe the main characters (CCSS ELA-Literacy-RL.3.3) and write an opinion piece related to the text.
>
> Sincerely,
>
> Awesome Teacher of Room 22

CHAPTER 7 | I Still Have Concerns, How Do I Move Forward?

You may also choose to notify your administrator so they are prepared for any parent concerns. Give them a few days' notice before reading the book about the topic in question. Share your instructional rationale so that the administrator can explain it if asked by parents. Below is an example. (Guidelines can be found in Tool 7.2.)

> Dear Principal,
>
> This email is to let you know that next week in class we will be reading a book about a transgender student. I will be sending an email to students' parents/guardians to let them know, and to give them the opportunity to read the book and ask questions in advance. We will read the picture book *Call Me Max* (2019) by Kyle Lukoff. The main character was born a girl and self-identifies as transgender. Told from the child's perspective, the book explains what it means to be transgender, explores gender-related bullying, and addresses identity development.
>
> There has been a lot of talk among my students recently about what boys and girls "should" do, such as how they should dress, what activities they should engage in, etc. Students are being bullied on the playground for these types of issues and it's important that we have a frank discussion about it to develop understanding, kindness, and empathy. As with all texts used in our classroom, this text will help us address our Grade 3 standards. Students will describe the main characters (CCSS ELA-Literacy-RL.3.3) and write an opinion piece related to the text.
>
> Thank you for your support.
>
> Sincerely,
>
> Awesome Teacher of Room 22

Bringing parents or community members into the school who can speak to the content of the book from a personal perspective is another possible solution. You can also consider how strongly a book addresses a particular issue and find one with a softer touch. For example, *King for a Day* by Rukhsana Khan normalizes children with physical dis/abilities; the main character in that book is also a child of color. These books are just as important as books that address issues of diversity more directly.

3. "What if I don't handle students' responses or questions well?

Problem: In this situation, you want to use diverse books but are concerned about your ability to handle students' responses or facilitate student discussions. You might be concerned about your students or yourself using inappropriate, disrespectful language. Language changes rather quickly, and you do not know what stereotypes students hear at home and might repeat at school.

It is important to remember that we all make mistakes. If you make a mistake, name it, apologize for it, and move on.

Possible Solutions: It is important to remember that we all make mistakes and to address those mistakes—whether yours or your students'—from a place of love. If it is your mistake, name it, apologize for it, do better, and move on. If it is a student's mistake, correct it immediately but kindly, provide the appropriate language, and move on.

You might consider using a sticky note to remind you of a term you want to use. Try keeping it where only you can see it, such as in the inside cover of the book during a read-aloud. Then, instead of searching in your head for the term you want to use (for example, *partner* rather than *wife* or *husband*), you'll have it right there in front of you.

You can also let the class know what you are working on and invite them to help keep you accountable. We have done this with the expression "you guys." We have shared with the class that we are working on using "you all" instead of "you guys," because we want to be more gender neutral in our language. The class lovingly catches our slips, and subsequently they begin using more gender neutral language as well.

4. "I'm not personally comfortable with the topic."

Problem: We are often uncomfortable with things that are not familiar. And with so many different issues of diversity, there are going to be topics that are unfamiliar, and likely uncomfortable, to all of us. Additionally, some topics, such as LGBTQ+ and even some different religions, can be taboo, depending on the context and the individual.

Possible Solutions: Get as comfortable as possible and then push yourself over that last hump simply because you love your students. It is likely that you will have an Islamic or Hindu student, or a student who is already questioning their gender or sexual preferences. Yes, this happens as early as kindergarten, or even earlier (Keating, 2015; Ryan et al., 2013).

Initial steps might be to read more about the topic, with a sharp eye toward positive role models. Are there any famous gay scientists? Do they have autobiographies? Once you have a basic understanding of a topic, you may choose to seek out organizations or individuals who can help. Through formal or informal personal networks, you will likely find someone who is willing to tell you about their lived experience. Note that in doing this, you are putting a significant onus on this person, so respect and gratitude are required. If they want to help you learn, great. If not, accept and respect their decision and find another way to learn.

> "Get as comfortable as possible and then push yourself over that last hump simply because you love your students."

An important part of this work involves self-reflection. We suggest setting aside time to identify and work through your discomfort by looking inward. The fact that you are reading this book tells us that you are open to learning more about how to engage with diverse texts in your classroom. Remember that you are exposing students to different social perspectives just like you expose them to topics in math and science. You are not indoctrinating them. You are providing alternative perspectives.

The following are some questions that may be helpful to guide your self-reflection so that you work through remaining discomfort with using diverse texts.

- What topic or topics are you uncomfortable with?

- What is difficult or concerning to you when you think about integrating texts on this topic in your classroom? List all difficulties or concerns that come to mind.

- What are some benefits that may develop if you integrate texts on this topic in your classroom? List all that come to mind.

- Consider your lists of concerns and benefits side by side. What do your lists tell you about your sticking points? What do your lists tell you about your motivation to do this work?

- Take a look at your list of concerns and consider them one by one. Does the concern call for learning more about the topic and community? Or working through deep-seated childhood, religious, or other beliefs that have shaped your view? Ask yourself: What am I willing to try?

We have provided Tool 7.1, Where Is My Resistance Coming From?, as an additional resource to help you work through your feelings about using diverse texts with your students.

CHAPTER 7 | I Still Have Concerns, How Do I Move Forward?

See It Through Their Eyes: Adult and Young Adult Texts for Diversity

Reading or listening to audiobooks written by diverse authors can also help ease you into different ways of storytelling and perspectives. Here is a brief list of some of the Adult and Young Adult texts we've been reading. We hope the books in this list will not only be enjoyable reads, but will also help you see the world through a different lens.

- *Pachinko* by Min Jin Lee
- *Red at the Bone* by Jacqueline Woodson
- *Shooting Kabul* by N. H. Senzai (historical fiction/memoir)
- *The Vanishing Half: A Novel* by Brit Bennett
- *The Curious Incident of the Dog in the Night-Time* by Mark Haddon
- *There There* by Tommy Orange
- *The Sympathizer: A Novel* by Viet Thanh Nguyen
- *Felix Ever After* by Kacen Callender (YA)
- *The Poet X* by Elizabeth Acevedo (YA)
- *The Hate U Give* by Angie Thomas (YA)
- *When I Was Puerto Rican: A Memoir* by Esmeralda Santiago (autobiography)
- *Rainbow Boys* by Alex Sanchez (YA)
- *Aristotle and Dante Discover the Secrets of the Universe* by Benjamin Alire Sáenz (YA)
- *All American Boys* by Jason Reynolds and Brendan Kiely (YA)
- *The Nickel Boys* or *The Underground Railroad* by Colson Whitehead
- *Braiding Sweetgrass: Indigenous Wisdom, Scientific Knowledge, and the Teachings of Plants* by Robin Wall Kimmerer
- *Killers of the Flower Moon: The Osage Murders and the Birth of the FBI* by David Grann
- *The Sentence, The Night Watchman,* or *The Round House* by Louise Erdrich

5. **I'm a person from a historically minoritized group. What if people think I'm teaching about this topic simply because I'm part of this group?**

Problem: In this situation, you are a teacher who is part of the marginalized group you wish to discuss. You feel self-conscious and do not want to appear self-serving or self-indulgent.

Possible Solutions: First, your story and those of others like you are valid, valuable, and deserve to be part of the curriculum. It's that simple. Students deserve to learn about different perspectives, and they are likely to be even more engaged if their teacher is part of a group they are learning about.

If you are still concerned about how it might be perceived by the adults around you, you can make the argument that your curriculum represents a range of diverse perspectives and groups. Your perspective is one of them. While you might be an insider for a particular book or unit, you will likely be an outsider for another part of the curriculum.

Bringing issues of race, gender, sexuality, religion, dis/ability, and social class into our classrooms requires that we do the self-work to identify and conquer our personal biases and resistance. In addition, it often requires overcoming some "adult issues," including other adults' perceptions of our teaching. It enables us to become more self-aware and therefore better advocates for all our students.

> **Quick Tip**
>
> Talking to other teachers about how they handle these issues might help you feel more comfortable. These conversations can also help you find like-minded colleagues to build a network for support and planning.

CHAPTER 7 | I Still Have Concerns, How Do I Move Forward?

> **Read this!**
>
> Kendi, I. X. (2019). *How to be an antiracist*. One World. While a number of books about race and racism have been published lately, we recommend this one due to its clarity and content.
>
> *Let's Talk!* This booklet from Learning for Justice addresses how to discuss race and other topics with children. It is free and accessible at https://www.learningforjustice.org/sites/default/files/general/TT%20Difficult%20Conversations%20web.pdf

The Time Is Now

We have hopefully succeeded in persuading you that students are never too young to address relevant issues of diversity in our classrooms. We have also hopefully shown you a path that just involves putting one foot in front of the other to begin this journey. Yes, some discomfort is inevitable, as a natural part of growth, but do not shy away from it. Acknowledge it, accept it, and help your students do the same. Congratulate and love yourself for the work you are doing, while simultaneously remembering that there is more to be done. Learning to implement culturally sustaining practices will be an ongoing process that will evolve as your students change from year to year, and even as they develop across a single year. This dynamism makes the work engaging and rewarding. And, most importantly, your students will benefit.

Just recently, we were speaking with one of our pre-service teachers and she shared how she began using diverse texts in her training class. Her mentor teacher observed her and followed suit in her own teaching. Soon, the entire grade-level team was ignited. Teachers were incorporating entire units that centered on historical figures of color. This small step grew into a mini-movement to create a fuller and more inclusive vision of the United States. The fact that you chose this book as a part of your development means a similar destiny, and beyond, awaits you and the students who learn with you.

> *"Bringing issues of race, gender, sexuality, religion, dis/ability, and social class into our classrooms requires that we do the self-work to identify and conquer our personal biases and resistance."*

We sincerely hope that these pages provide the support you need to actively deconstruct in your classroom race, gender, dis/ability, sexual orientation, and other topics that have generally been excluded from schools. Enabling students to see themselves represented in school—by being reflected and respected in the curriculum—shows them that they, too, belong. Their stories and lives are also important. They, too, are loved. School is not only for one group of students. Instead, your students *are* the school. Schools would be empty buildings without them. Your students—their full selves with multiple identities—are the world.

Enabling students to see themselves represented in the curriculum shows them that they, too, belong. Their stories and their lives are also important.

Tools to Try

The tools in this chapter are designed to help educators and students' families overcome resistance to the use of diverse texts in the classroom. Tool 7.1 will help with self-reflection. And, while we can't shift anyone else's beliefs, we can help them understand and respect our instructional decisions. Tool 7.2 will help you communicate with families and administrators about your decision to use diverse texts.

Tool 7.1 Where Is My Resistance Coming From?

Use this tool to help you think more deeply about your own background and internalized biases that might be getting in the way of your journey. Self-reflection is critical for teaching in general, but even more important when it comes to topics of diversity. This tool can be used anytime you notice discomfort or reluctance around a topic related to inclusive, anti-racist teaching. Honor your willingness to self-reflect and keep self-compassion at the forefront of your mind when using this tool.

School is not only for one group of students. Instead, your students *are* the school.

Tool 7.1 Where Is My Resistance Coming From?

Self-Reflection Questions	My Answers
What topics am I comfortable talking and reading about with my students?	
What topics are harder for me? What has been my experience with these topics?	
What does my community think of these topics? How do I know?	
What do I think? Why do I think it?	
What are my concerns? What do I think might happen if I read/talk about this topic with students?	
How might I learn more about this topic? What books, organizations, or online resources might be available?	
Whom might I talk to?	
What are my immediate next steps to become more comfortable with this topic?	
What are my longer-term next steps?	

CHAPTER 7 | I Still Have Concerns, How Do I Move Forward?

Tool 7.2 Guidelines for Communicating with Families and Administrators

This tool provides guidance on how to communicate with families and administrators about your inclusion of diverse texts. Letting *families* (parents, guardians, older siblings, grandparents, or other caregivers) know in advance that a particularly sensitive topic will be discussed in class is helpful because they have time to think about how to address the issue if their child asks about it at home. Similarly, alerting *administrators* before using books about particularly controversial topics is important because it enables them to be prepared if a parent/guardian speaks to them about it.

While we can't shift anyone else's beliefs, we can help administrators and caregivers understand our instructional decisions.

Tool 7.2 Guidelines for Communicating with Families and Administrators

- Use a written form of communication (email, note, etc.).
- Include the standard and learning objective to be addressed.
- Include the title of the book, author, and topic(s) it addresses.
- Describe how or why it is important to address the book's topic with your students.
- Do not include educational jargon.
- Remind families that you have established norms or expectations to ensure respect for all perspectives.
- Keep it short and simple.
- Welcome questions or comments and offer families/caregivers access to the book.

Voices from the Field

Ruth Torres
teacher

"If we want to be effective teachers, we need to be open. We have to let our students know that they are welcomed."

Ruth Torres, a Latinx sixth-grade bilingual teacher in Ceres Unified School District in Ceres, California, has been teaching for four years. Ruth remembers the first time she felt nervous about engaging with diverse literature in her teacher education program. She was learning that diversity was much more than race, ethnicity, and language. She said, "One of the topics that for me was touchy and difficult was the gay community. I was nervous every time we would talk about it, mainly because I grew up in a conservative religious family." She said, "I was raised thinking one thing, and then I was learning a different thing." She was open to learning because her teacher education program emphasized inclusivity, love, support, and seeing students as individuals.

Ruth found learning how to integrate texts with LGBTQ+ characters and themes difficult, yet she realized the need for these texts when she entered the classroom. At the beginning of the year, she asked students to share photographs of their family and she began to see that students were bringing in photos with two moms or two dads. She wanted all of her students to feel loved and welcomed as they are; this pushed her to work on overcoming her nervousness.

She said, "First, I read more about these communities. I looked at different books. I talked to different people, not only my colleagues, but also classmates at that time. I talked with people around me who deeply know about the topic or about diverse students. After that, I talked to two different administrators at my school. I had really good, supportive people in administration. One of the coaches at my school said, 'You know what, let's just talk about it. Tell me what you feel. Tell me how you feel. And then, I can give you my advice.' And that's what happened."

Ruth ultimately decided to include books reflecting the LGBTQ+ community in her classroom and to engage her students in discussions. After her decision, Ruth still had to work to overcome her nervousness to use the books and open up discussions with students. She said, "I tried to learn as much as possible about each topic that I wanted to talk about with my students. I practiced with my family, talking to them about these topics. Sometimes my family members would make jokes about some topics. And I would remind them that this was a time for me to practice saying, 'Hey, I don't think this is appropriate' or 'Why do you think that?' And then I would open that discussion at the table." She described herself taking deep breaths and preparing with notes about points she wanted to make with her students. Ruth added, "Because this is all about planning. I prepared myself mentally to talk about the issues."

Ruth understands that engaging students with diverse texts can be challenging for teachers. If teachers do not yet feel prepared to engage in certain topics, she encourages them to just say, "I'm not sure. Let me think about it. Let me read, do more research." She emphasizes that teachers should leave the door open for future discussions if they are not ready and to make sure that they follow through with additional reading and research. Ruth concluded with the following reflection: "If we want to be effective teachers, we need to be open. We have to let our students know that they are welcomed.... And every teacher will be ready at different times and in different ways. Students are looking for allies, for people who are on their side to trust. Teachers are key."

Voices from the Field

Sarita Sundaram
teacher

"When the students presented on topics of diversity, I invited school board members to Zoom in."

A few years ago, Sarita was trying Culturally Responsive Teaching practices in her classroom. Part of it included teaching United States history. She shared, "My principal, who observed my lessons multiple times, asked me, 'Why are you teaching about slavery? That happened a long time ago. Why are you teaching about 9/11? Doesn't it make people feel uncomfortable?' There were Muslim students in my class. And we talked about 9/11, and what happened after that, including the racial profiling. My principal said, 'It sounds like you're turning everybody against mainstream America, or against being patriotic.' This principal has a lot of respect for me. So I explained it to him, and because he respected my work, it was fine."

She added, "Now our district is going through this anti-racist journey. We are part of a book club figuring out this anti-racist learning together. On one occasion, he apologized for the past comment, saying, 'Sorry, I completely get it now.'"

Sarita continued, "When the students presented on topics of diversity, I invited school board members to Zoom in. They listened to the presentations, and then they gave the students a shout-out during their next board meeting."

"Know that these conversations are not going to be easy. Know that you have a lot to learn."

Michelle Rosas-Gonzalez
teacher

Michelle Rosas-Gonzalez shared an important conversation she had with a student's mother after reading *And Tango Makes Three* by Justin Richardson and Peter Parnell. Tango is about two male penguins who were in love and raised a chick together. Michelle recounted, "A student's mom said the book made her uncomfortable. I told the mom, 'We read the story to make everybody feel safe. We know that we have families with two moms at our school. We have to create a safe space and include everybody as much as possible.' It was really hard to have that conversation." However, the conversation went well and the mom understood.

Michelle noted that she should have communicated with families in advance. "That was on me," she said. "Transparency is important." Michelle explained that she now communicates with families and her administrator regularly about diverse books she will use.

She suggests, "Know that these conversations are not going to be easy. Know that you have a lot to learn. Always ground yourself in why you're doing this—to honor students and to create a safe space for all of them. Know that you don't know everything, that you are learning just as much as your students are. And once you know better, do better."

CHAPTER 7 | I Still Have Concerns, How Do I Move Forward?

A Lifelong Journey

Throughout this book, we have included a variety of exceptional educators' voices so that you can hear directly from teachers engaged in this work. They have shared their very personal and real challenges in creating **conscious classrooms.** They recognize that the time is now and are identifying and conquering their internal resistance. Ruth shared her personal struggle with her own family members' beliefs. Sarita shared her conversations with her principal as she helped him see the importance of teaching diverse historical perspectives. Michelle shared about her experience with a parent and what she learned about the importance of transparency going forward.

You will likely navigate similar concerns as you consider your own beliefs and biases, learn about your school's and community's norms and expectations, and reflect on best practices for addressing diverse students' needs. Consider who you are and what you stand for. While teachers are required to follow content standards, teaching is not standardized. Who you are and what you stand for makes its way into your teaching practice in what you do and do not do, what you say and do not say. As a teacher, you are a role model. What do you want to model? Can you be the kind of teacher you want to be at your current site? Think about support from your administration, from your colleagues, and from families at your site. Who might be your allies in this work? Or is a change necessary in order to become the kind of teacher you want to be?

We each have been doing this work for about two decades, and we continue to reflect on these questions and push ourselves to do better each day, with each group of students, and in conversations with colleagues, administrators, policy makers, and others. We hope you now have a greater sense of urgency and feel better prepared to join us in this lifelong journey to serve children and make our schools more inclusive, equitable, and just.

Last Words

We leave you with these last words. At the risk of you rolling your eyes, we are going to say again:

> This is hard work. You will encounter resistance. You will need to make difficult decisions. You will make mistakes. Learn from them, do better, and do it anyway.

We hope that you have come to understand that business as usual in many classrooms presents White, middle-class, English-monolingual, able-bodied, heteronormative people as "normal" and people deviating from that as "less than." Even if you have the best of intentions, business as usual causes harm.

Instead, join us in creating **Conscious Classrooms**.

Drs. Claudia Rodriguez-Mojica and Allison Briceño

APPENDIX

Helpful Websites for Identifying Diverse Books

Website	What It Is and Does
Learning for Justice https://www.learningforjustice.org/	Learning for Justice seeks to help teachers and schools educate children and youth to be active participants in a diverse democracy. It has a plethora of resources for Grades K–12.
Teaching for Change https://www.teachingforchange.org/	Teaching for Change provides teachers and parents with the tools to create schools where students learn to read, write, and change the world.
Social Justice Books https://socialjusticebooks.org/	Social Justice Books vets and promotes social justice books, and includes reviews. It is a project of Teaching for Change.
Diverse BookFinder™ https://diversebookfinder.org/	Diverse BookFinder™ has a searchable collection of children's picture books featuring Black and Indigenous people and People of Color (BIPOC). The site has cataloged diverse trade picture books published since 2002.
Colours of Us https://coloursofus.com/multicultural-childrens-books-lists/	Colours of Us has a searchable diverse children's book database and logs for additional information and book collections.

Use the following **Observation Tool for Discussions About Diversity** to assess students' growth over time. Simply put a check mark in each student's column when behaviors in the first column are observed. Multiple check marks can signify that the behavior was observed multiple times. Alternatively, you can use a plus sign (+) when the student meets criteria or a minus sign (–) for comments that miss the mark.

Note that we included diversity-related criteria at the top, followed by sections on content expectations and general expectations. You can use one or all of these sections. You can adjust this tool based on your goals and students' needs by changing or adding behaviors you would like to observe. Maintaining observational notes helps you assess students and plan future lessons based on data. This tool is currently set up for small-group observation but can easily be adapted for larger groups or whole-class discussions.

Observation Tool for Discussions About Diversity

	Student 1	Student 2	Student 3	Student 4	Student 5	Student 6
Diversity Expectations						
Student used language from the prompting cards appropriately.						
Student adapted ideas from the prompting cards and used their own (appropriate) language.						
Student questioned another student's thinking or appropriately challenged them.						
Student identified whose story was being told and whose was not.						
Student demonstrated understanding of or empathy toward a character different from themselves.						
[add your own criteria]						
Content Expectations						
Student connected their idea to a previous comment or question.						
Student used evidence from the text to support their argument.						
Student's comment showed critical or inferential reading of the text.						
Student made an insightful connection to the text.						
Student used content vocabulary appropriately. (Note words used.)						
[add your own criteria]						
General Expectations						
Student was on task and focused.						
[add your own criteria]						
Misunderstandings about the content to come back to:						
Notes about students' content knowledge, comprehension, language use, or other:						

Introduction
Literature Cited

Hoffman, M. (1991). *Amazing Grace*. Dial Books.

Roy, A. (2008). *The god of small things: A novel.* Random House.

References

Alfaro, C. (2019). Preparing critically conscious dual-language teachers: Recognizing and interrupting dominant ideologies. *Theory Into Practice, 58*(2), 194–203.

Arce, J. (2004). Latino bilingual teachers: The struggle to sustain an emancipatory pedagogy in public schools. *International Journal of Qualitative Studies in Education, 17*(2), 227–246. https://doi.org/10.1080/0951839031000 1653880

Briceño, A., Rodriguez-Mojica, C., & Muñoz-Muñoz, E. (2018). From English learner to Spanish learner: Raciolinguistic beliefs that influence heritage Spanish speaking teacher candidates. *Language and Education, 32*(3), 212–226.

Brito, I., Lima, A., & Auerbach, E. (2004). The logic of nonstandard teaching: A course in Cape Verdean language, culture and history. In B. Norton & K. Toohey (Eds.), *Critical pedagogies and language learning* (pp. 181–200). Cambridge University Press.

California Department of Education. (2019). *Fingertip facts on education in California.* https://www.cde.ca.gov/ds/sd/cb/ceffingertipfacts.asp

Compton-Lilly, C., & Nayan, R. (2016). Literacy capital in two immigrant families: Longitudinal case studies. In P. Ruggiano Schmidt & A. M. Lazar (Eds.), *Reconceptualizing literacy in the new age of multiculturalism and pluralism, 2nd edition* (pp. 191–214). Information Age Publishing.

Freire, P. (1987). *Education for critical consciousness.* Continuum Publishing.

Geiger, A. W. (2018, August 27). America's public school teachers are far less racially and ethnically diverse than their students. Pew Research Center.

Goodley, D., & Runswick-Cole, K. (2016). Becoming dishuman: Thinking about the human through dis/ability. *Discourse: Studies in the Cultural Politics of Education, 37*(1), 1–15.

Hattie, J. (2012). *Visible learning for teachers: Maximizing impact on learning.* Routledge.

Jones, S. (2004). Living poverty and literacy learning: Sanctioning topics of students' lives. *Language Arts, 81*(6), 461–469.

Kendi, I. X. (2019). *How to be an antiracist.* One World.

Love, B. L. (2019). *We want to do more than survive: Abolitionist teaching and the pursuit of educational freedom.* Beacon Press.

Moll, L. C., Amanti, C., Neff, D., & Gonzalez, N. (1992). Funds of knowledge for teaching: Using a qualitative approach to connect homes and classrooms. *Theory Into Practice, 31*(2), 132–141.

National Center for Education Statistics. (2021). *Fast facts.* https://nces.ed.gov/programs/coe/indicator/cge

Palmer, D. K., Cervantes-Soon, C., Dorner, L., & Heiman, D. (2019). Bilingualism, biliteracy, biculturalism, and critical consciousness for all: Proposing a fourth fundamental goal for two-way dual language education. *Theory Into Practice, 58*(2), 121–133.

Picower, B. (2009). The unexamined whiteness of teaching: How white teachers maintain and enact dominant racial ideologies. *Race, Ethnicity, and Education, 12*(2), 197–215.

Riley, K., & Crawford-Garrett, K. (2016). Critical texts in literacy teacher education: Living inquiries into racial justice and immigration. *Language Arts, 94*(2), 94–107.

Rodriguez-Mojica, C. (2018). From test scores to language use: Emergent bilinguals using English to accomplish academic tasks. *International Multilingual Research Journal, 12*(1), 31–61.

Rodriguez-Mojica, C., & Briceño, A. (2018). Sentence stems that support reading comprehension. *The Reading Teacher, 72*(3), 398–402.

Ryan, C. L., & Hermann-Wilmarth, J. M. (2018). *Reading the rainbow: LGBTQ-inclusive literacy instruction in the elementary classroom.* Teachers College Press.

Singleton, G. E. (2014). *Courageous conversations about race: A field guide for achieving equity in schools* (2nd ed.). Corwin.

U.S. Department of Education Office for Civil Rights. (2014). *Civil rights data collection: Data snapshot (school discipline)*. https://www2.ed.gov/about/offices/list/ocr/docs/crdc-discipline-snapshot.pdf

Yang, J. L., Anyon, Y., Pauline, M., Wiley, K. E., Cash, D., Downing, B. J., Greer, E., Kelty, E., Morgan, T. L., & Pisciotta, L. (2018). "We have to educate every single student, not just the ones that look like us": Support service providers' beliefs about the root causes of the school-to-prison pipeline for youth of color. *Equity & Excellence in Education, 51*(3–4), 316–331. https://doi.org/10.1080/10665684.2018.1539358

Yosso, T. J. (2005). Whose culture has capital? A critical race theory discussion of community cultural wealth. *Race, Ethnicity, and Education, 8*(1), 69–91. https://doi.org/10.1080/1361332052000341006

Chapter 1
Literature Cited

Adeyoha, K., & Adeyoha, A. (2017). *47,000 beads*. Flamingo Rampant.

Averbeck, J., & Ismail, Y. (2015). *One word from Sophia*. Atheneum Books for Young Readers.

Borucki, R. (2021). *Zara's big messy day (that turned out okay)*. Wheat Penny Press.

Bruchac, J. (2019). *The powwow thief*. Reycraft Books.

de la Peña, M. (2018). *Love*. G. P. Putnam's Sons Books for Young Readers.

Ewert, M. (2008). *10,000 dresses*. Seven Stories Press.

Gonzales, M. (2017). *Yo soy Muslim: A father's letter to his daughter*. Simon & Schuster.

González, R. (2016). *Antonio's card/La tarjeta de Antonio*. Lee & Low Books.

Hutchins, P. (1989). *The doorbell rang*. Greenwillow Books.

Khaki, E-F., & Jackson, T. (2017). *Moondragon in the mosque garden*. Flamingo Rampant.

Khan, R. (2014). *King for a day*. Lee & Low Books.

Liu, C., & Chiang, I-T. (2020). *Woodpecker girl*. Reycraft Books.

Olsen, S. (2020). *Our class is a family*. Shannon Olsen.

Penfold, A. (2018). *All are welcome*. Knopf Books for Young Readers.

Rivas, L. (2018). *They call me Mix/Me llaman Maestre*. Lourdes Rivas.

Singh, B., & Ji, G. A. D. (2018). *Ajeet Singh: The invincible lion*. Brave Lion Books.

Tarpley, N. A. (2001). *I love my hair!* Little, Brown & Company.

Tonatiuh, D. (2013). *Pancho Rabbit and the coyote: A migrant's tale*. Abrams.

Wood, D. (2009). *Miss Little's gift*. Candlewick Press.

Woodson, J. (2018). *The day you begin*. Nancy Paulsen Books.

References

Cooperative Children's Book Center, School of Education, University of Wisconsin–Madison. (2021). *Books by and/or about Black, Indigenous and People of Color (all years)*. [Statistics]. https://ccbc.education.wisc.edu/literature-resources/ccbc-diversity-statistics/books-by-about-poc-fnn/

Fishman-Weaver, K. (2019, December 3). *How to audit your classroom library for diversity*. Edutopia. https://www.edutopia.org/article/how-audit-your-classroom-library-diversity

Iwai, Y. (2015). Using multicultural children's literature to teach diverse perspectives. *Kappa Delta Pi Record, 51*(2), 81–86.

Johnson, N. J., Koss, M. D., & Martinez, M. (2018). Through the sliding glass door: #EmpowerTheReader. *The Reading Teacher, 71*(5), 569–577.

Muhammad, G. (2020). *Cultivating genius: An equity framework for culturally and historically responsive literacy*. Scholastic Inc.

Pennell, A. E., Wollak, B., & Koppenhaver, D. A. (2018). Respectful representations of disability in picture books. *The Reading Teacher, 71*(4), 411–419.

Chapter 2
Literature Cited

Alexie, S. (2009). *The absolutely true diary of a part-time Indian*. Little, Brown and Company.

Boelts, M. (2009). *Those shoes*. Candlewick.

Blume, J. (1986). *Are you there God? It's me, Margaret*. Yearling.

Blume, J. (2007). *Tales of a fourth grade nothing*. Puffin Books.

Gipson, F. (1995). *Old Yeller*. HarperCollins.

Martin, A. M. (1997). *The baby-sitters club*. Scholastic.

References

Alim, H. S., & Paris, D. (2017). What is culturally sustaining pedagogy and why does it matter? In D. Paris & H. S. Alim (Eds.), *Culturally sustaining pedagogies: Teaching and learning for justice in a changing world* (pp. 1–24). Teachers College Press.

Bishop, R. S. (1990). Mirrors, windows, and sliding glass doors. *Perspectives*, 6(3), ix–xi.

Christ, T., Chiu, M. M., Rider, S., Kitson, D., Hanser, K., McConnell, E., Dipzinski, R., & Mayernik, H. (2018). Cultural relevance and informal reading inventory performance: African-American primary and middle school students. *Literacy Research and Instruction*, 57(2), 117–134.

Gray, E. S. (2009). The importance of visibility: Students' and teachers' criteria for selecting African American literature. *The Reading Teacher*, 62(6), 472–481.

Irizarry, J. G. (2017). "For us, by us": A vision for culturally sustaining pedagogies forwarded by Latinx youth. In D. Paris & H. S. Alim (Eds.), *Culturally sustaining pedagogies: Teaching and learning for justice in a changing world* (pp. 83–98). Teachers College Press.

Kinloch, V., Burkhard, T., & Penn, C. (2017). When school is not enough: Understanding the lives and literacies of Black youth. *Research in the Teaching of English*, 34–54.

Ladson-Billings, G. (1994). Who will teach our children? Preparing teachers to successfully teach African American students. In E. R. Hollins, J. E. King, & W. C. Hayman (Eds.), *Teaching diverse populations: Formulating a knowledge base*, 129–142. State University of New York Press.

Ladson-Billings, G. (1995a). Toward a theory of culturally relevant pedagogy. *American Educational Research Journal*, 32(3), 465–491.

Ladson-Billings, G. (1995b). But that's just good teaching! The case for culturally relevant pedagogy. *Theory Into Practice*, 34(3), 159–165.

Ladson-Billings, G. (2014). Culturally relevant pedagogy 2.0: aka the remix. *Harvard Educational Review*, 84(1), 74–84.

Ladson-Billings, G. (2017). The (R)Evolution will not be standardized: Teacher education, hip-hop pedagogy, and culturally relevant pedagogy 2.0. In D. Paris & H. S. Alim (Eds.), *Culturally sustaining pedagogies: Teaching and learning for justice in a changing world* (pp. 141–156). Teachers College Press.

Lee, T. S., & McCarty, T. L. (2017). Upholding Indigenous education sovereignty through critical culturally sustaining/revitalizing pedagogy. In D. Paris & H. S. Alim (Eds.), *Culturally sustaining pedagogies: Teaching and learning for justice in a changing world* (pp. 61–82). Teachers College Press.

Meacham, S. J., Meacham, S., Thompson, M., & Graves, H. (2019). Hip-hop early literacy in K–1 classrooms. *The Reading Teacher*, 73(1), 29–37.

Muhammad, G. (2020). *Cultivating genius: An equity framework for culturally and historically responsive literacy*. Scholastic Inc.

Paris, D. (2012). Culturally sustaining pedagogy: A needed change in stance, terminology, and practice. *Educational Researcher*, 41(3), 93–97.

Paris, D., & Alim, H. S. (Eds.). (2017). *Culturally sustaining pedagogies: Teaching and learning for justice in a changing world*. Teachers College Press.

Wong, C., & Peña, C. (2017). Policing and performing culture: Rethinking "culture" and the role of the arts in culturally sustaining pedagogies. In D. Paris & H. S. Alim (Eds.), *Culturally sustaining pedagogies: Teaching and learning for justice in a changing world* (pp. 117–138). Teachers College Press.

Chapter 3
Literature Cited

Ada, A. F. (2019). *Abuelita's secret*. Reycraft Books.

Ahn, C. (2021). *A little book about activism*. A Kids' Book About.

Averbeck, J., & Ismail, Y. (2015). *One word from Sophia*. Atheneum Books for Young Readers.

Bergman, S. B. (2019). *Power poems for small humans*. Flamingo Rampant.

Bodach, V. (2020). *Little thief! Chota chor!* Reycraft Books.

Borucki, R. (2021). *Zara's big messy day (that turned out okay)*. Wheat Penny Press.

Bruchac, J. (2019). *The powwow thief*. Reycraft Books.

Cherry-Paul, S., Kendi, I. X., & Reynolds, J. (2021). *Stamped (for kids): Racism, antiracism, and you*. Little, Brown Books for Young Readers.

Colato Laínez, R. (2016). *Mamá the alien/Mamá la extraterrestre*. Lee & Low Books.

de la Peña, M. (2018). *Carmela full of wishes*. G. P. Putnam's Sons Books for Young Readers.

Heska Wanbli Weiden, D. (2019). *Spotted Tail*. Reycraft Books.

Hudson, W., & Hudson, C. W. (Eds.). (2019). *We rise, we resist, we raise our voices*. Yearling.

Kendi, I. X. (2020). *Antiracist baby*. Kokila.

Khan, R. (2014). *King for a day*. Lee & Low Books.

Kheiriyeh, R. (2020). *Bahar, the lucky*. Reycraft Books.

Love, J. (2018). *Julián is a mermaid*. Candlewick.

Lukoff, K. (2019). *Call me Max*. Reycraft Books.

Lukoff, K. (2019). *Max and the talent show*. Reycraft Books.

Lukoff, K. (2020). *Max on the farm*. Reycraft Books.

Morales, Y. (2018). *Dreamers*. Neal Porter Books.

Muhammad, I. (2019). *The proudest blue: A story of hijab and family*. Little, Brown Books for Young Readers.

Patel, S., & Haynes, E. (2015). *Ganesha's sweet tooth*. Chronicle Books.

Schachner, J. (2005). *Skippyjon Jones*. Puffin Books.

Woodson, J. (2018). *The day you begin*. Nancy Paulsen Books.

References

Allington, R. L. (2013). What really matters when working with struggling readers. *The Reading Teacher, 66*(7), 520–530.

Allington, R. L., & McGill-Franzen, A. (Eds.). (2018). *Summer reading: Closing the rich/poor reading achievement gap* (2nd ed.). Teachers College Press.

Derman-Sparks, L., & A.B.C. Task Force. (n.d.). Ten quick ways to analyze children's books for sexism and racism. https://www.teachingforchange.org/wp-content/uploads/2012/08/ec_tenquickways_english.pdf

Martínez-Roldán, C. M. (2013). The representation of Latinos and the use of Spanish: A critical content analysis of *Skippyjon Jones*. *Journal of Children's Literature, 39*(1), 5–14. https://login.libproxy.scu.edu/login?qurl=https%3A%2F%2Fwww.proquest.com%2Fscholarly-journals%2Frepresentation-latinos-use-spanish-critical%2Fdocview%2F1441673954%2Fse-2%3Faccountid%3D13679

Moreno, C. (2016, April 7). Is Speedy Gonzales a Mexican hero or a stereotype in cartoon form? *Huffington Post*. https://www.huffpost.com/entry/is-speedy-gonzales-a-mexican-hero-or-a-stereotype-in-cartoon-form_n_5706a852e4b0537661890eaa

Pugh, T. (2018). *The queer fantasies of the American family sitcom*. Rutgers University Press.

Schwartz, K. (2016, June 20). 20 books featuring diverse characters to inspire connection and empathy. *KQED*. https://www.kqed.org/mindshift/45121/20-books-featuring-diverse-characters-to-inspire-connection-and-empathy

Thomas, E. E. (2016). Stories still matter: Rethinking the role of diverse children's literature today. *Language Arts, 94*(2), 112–119.

Chapter 4
Literature Cited

de la Peña, M. (2018). *Carmela full of wishes*. G. P. Putnam's Sons Books for Young Readers.

Lázaro, G. (2020). *The legend of the coquí*. Reycraft Books.

Liu, C. & Chiang, I-T. (2020). *Woodpecker girl.* Reycraft Books.

Muñoz Ryan, P. (2000). *Esperanza rising.* Scholastic.

Young, E. (1989). *Lon Po Po: A Red-Riding Hood story from China.* Philomel Books.

References

Allington, R. L., & Gabriel, R. E. (2012). Every child, every day. *Educational Leadership, 69*(5), 10–15.

Francois, C. (2013). Reading is about relating: Urban youths give voice to the possibilities for school literacy. *Journal of Adolescent & Adult Literacy, 57*(2), 141–149.

Goodwin, P. (2017). Becoming a reluctant reader. In J. Court (Ed.), *Reading by right: Successful strategies to ensure every child can read to succeed* (pp. 33–50). Facet Publishing.

Gustafson, B. (2017, October 31). *Build better booktalks.* [Video]. YouTube. https://www.youtube.com/watch?app=desktop&v=kRkqjudkaME&feature=youtu.be

Gustafson, B. (2018, March 18). 2018 world championship of booktalks. In *The 30-second booktalk podcast.* [Video]. YouTube. https://www.youtube.com/watch?v=aVUVOAVqdcU&feature=emb_logo

Guthrie, J. T., & Humenick, N. M. (2004). Motivating students to read: Evidence for classroom practices that increase reading motivation and achievement. In P. McCardle & V. Chhabra (Eds.), *The voice of evidence in reading research* (pp. 329–354). Paul H. Brookes Publishing Co.

Ivey, G., & Broaddus, K. (2001). "Just plain reading": A survey of what makes students want to read in middle school classrooms. *Reading Research Quarterly, 36*(4), 350–377.

Muhammad, G. (2020). *Cultivating genius: An equity framework for culturally and historically responsive literacy.* Scholastic Inc.

National Governors Association Center for Best Practices & Council of Chief State School Officers. (2010). *Common Core State Standards.* Authors.

Palincsar, A. S., & Brown, A. L. (1984). Reciprocal teaching of comprehension-fostering and comprehension-monitoring activities. *Cognition and Instruction, 1*(2), 117–175.

Reis, S. M., McCoach, D. B., Coyne, M., Schreiber, F. J., Eckert, R. D., & Gubbins, E. J. (2007). Using planned enrichment strategies with direct instruction to improve reading fluency, comprehension, and attitude toward reading: An evidence-based study. *The Elementary School Journal, 108*(1), 3–23.

Chapter 5
Literature Cited

Alko, S. (2015). *The case for Loving: The fight for interracial marriage.* Arthur A. Levine Books.

Beaty, A. (2016). *Ada Twist, scientist.* Abrams Books for Young Readers.

Becker, H. (2018). *Counting on Katherine: How Katherine Johnson saved Apollo 13.* Henry Holt & Co.

Brown, M. (2020). *Side by side/Lado a lado: The story of Dolores Huerta and Cesar Chavez/La historia de Dolores Huerta y César Chávez.* HarperCollins.

Colato Laínez, R. (2016). *Mamá the alien/Mamá la extraterrestre.* Lee & Low Books.

Crespo, A. (2020). *Lia & Luís: Who has more?* Charlesbridge.

de la Peña, M. (2018). *Carmela full of wishes.* G. P. Putnam's Sons Books for Young Readers.

Deutsch, S. (2017). *Girls who code.* Penguin Workshop.

Domenzain, A. (2021). *For all/Para todos.* Hard Ball Press.

Harrington, J. N. (2019). *Buzzing with questions: The inquisitive mind of Charles Henry Turner.* Calkins Creek.

Johnson, K., Hylick, J., & Moore, K. (2021). *One step further: My story of math, the moon, and a lifelong mission.* National Geographic Kids.

Jordan-Fenton, C., & Pokiak-Fenton, M. (2013). *When I was eight.* Annick Press.

Khan, R. (2014). *King for a day.* Lee & Low Books.

Krull, K. (2003). *Harvesting hope: The story of Cesar Chavez.* Houghton Mifflin Harcourt Books for Young Readers.

Lawlor, L. (2014). *Rachel Carson and her book that changed the world.* Holiday House.

Levine, E. (2007). *Henry's freedom box: A true story from the Underground Railroad*. Scholastic Press.

Levinson, C. (2017). *The youngest marcher: The story of Audrey Faye Hendricks, a young civil rights activist*. Atheneum Books for Young Readers.

Lindstrom, C. (2020). *We are water protectors*. Roaring Brook Press.

Mochizuki, K. (2018). *Baseball saved us*. Lee & Low Books.

Morales, A. (2021). *Areli is a Dreamer: A true story*. Random House Studio.

Morales, Y. (2018). *Dreamers*. Neal Porter Books.

Mosca, J. F. (2018). *The girl with a mind for math: The story of Raye Montague*. The Innovation Press.

National Governors Association Center for Best Practices & Council of Chief State School Officers. (2010). *Common Core State Standards*. Authors.

NGSS Lead States. (2013). *Next Generation Science Standards*. https://www.nextgenscience.org/

Paul, M. (2015). *One plastic bag: Isatou Ceesay and the recycling women of the Gambia*. Millbrook Press.

Pimentel, A. B. (2020). *All the way to the top: How one girl's fight for Americans with disabilities changed everything*. Sourcebooks Explore.

Pinkney, A. D. (2013). *Let it shine: Stories of Black women freedom fighters*. Clarion Books.

Rogers, A. L. (2020). *Mary and the Trail of Tears: A Cherokee removal survival story*. Capstone Press.

Sanders, R. (2018). *Pride: The story of Harvey Milk and the rainbow flag*. Random House.

Schachner, J. (2005). *Skippyjon Jones*. Puffin Books.

Shetterly, M. L. (2018). *Hidden figures: The true story of four Black women and the space race*. HarperCollins.

Simon, A. (2018). *Abby invents unbreakable crayons*. Bella Agnes Books.

Sorell, T. (2021). *We are still here!: Native American truths everyone should know*. Charlesbridge.

Soto, G. (1997). *Chato's kitchen*. Puffin Books.

Southern Poverty Law Center. (2018, June 27). *Small truths: The immigration experience through the eyes of children*. [Video]. YouTube. https://www.youtube.com/watch?v=-v28soJ0DOc&ab_channel=DescribedandCaptionedMediaProgram

Spires, A. (2013). *The most magnificent thing*. Kids Can Press.

Suneby, E. (2018). *Iqbal and his ingenious idea: How a science project helps one family and the planet*. Kids Can Press.

Tate, D. (2020). *William Still and his freedom stories: The father of the Underground Railroad*. Peachtree Publishing Company.

Tonatiuh, D. (2014). *Separate is never equal: Sylvia Mendez and her family's fight for desegregation*. Harry N. Abrams.

Uchida, Y. (1996). *The bracelet*. Puffin Books.

Warren, S. (2012). *Dolores Huerta: A hero to migrant workers*. Two Lions.

Williams, K. L. (1990). *Galimoto*. HarperCollins.

Winter, J. (2017). *The world is not a rectangle: A portrait of architect Zaha Hadid*. Beach Lane Books.

Woodson, J. (2001). *The other side*. G. P. Putnam's Sons.

References

Brown, B. A. (2019). *Science in the city: Culturally relevant STEM education*. Harvard Education Press.

Colwell, J. (2019). Selecting texts for disciplinary literacy instruction. *The Reading Teacher, 72*(5), 631–637.

Muhammad, G. (2020). *Cultivating genius: An equity framework for culturally and historically responsive literacy*. Scholastic Inc.

Picower, B. (2012). Using their words: Six elements of social justice curriculum design for the elementary classroom. *International Journal of Multicultural Education, 14*(1), 1–17.

Chapter 6
Literature Cited

Genhart, M. (2018). *Love is love*. Little Pickle Press.

References

Hagerman, M. A. (2019). Conversations with kids about race. *Phi Delta Kappan, 100*(7), 17–21.

Kay, M. R. (2018). *Not light, but fire: How to lead meaningful race conversations in the classroom.* Stenhouse Publishers.

Chapter 7
Literature Cited

Khan, R. (2014). *King for a day.* Lee & Low Books.

Lukoff, K. (2019). *Call me Max.* Reycraft Books.

Richardson, J., & Parnell, P. (2015). *And Tango makes three.* Little Simon.

References

Acevedo, E. (2020). *The poet X.* Quill Tree Books.

Bennett, B. (2021). *The vanishing half: A novel.* Penguin US.

Bronski, M. (2011). *A queer history of the United States* (Vol. 1). Beacon Press.

Callender, K. (2021). *Felix ever after.* Balzer & Bray.

Dunbar-Ortiz, R. (2014). *An Indigenous peoples' history of the United States* (Vol. 3). Beacon Press.

Erdrich, L. (2013). *The Round House.* Harper Perennial.

Erdrich, L. (2021). *The night watchman.* Harper Perennial.

Erdrich, L. (2021). *The sentence.* Harper.

Grann, D. (2017). *Killers of the flower moon: The Osage murders and the birth of the FBI.* Doubleday.

Haddon, M. (2004). *The curious incident of the dog in the night-time.* Vintage Contemporaries.

Hagerman, M. A. (2019). Conversations with kids about race. *Phi Delta Kappan, 100*(7), 17–21.

Keating, S. (2015, April 27). *Coming out as gay in elementary school.* BuzzFeedNews. https://www.buzzfeednews.com/article/shannonkeating/coming-out-as-gay-in-elementary-school

Kendi, I. X. (2019). *How to be an antiracist.* One World.

Kimmerer, R. W. (2013). *Braiding sweetgrass: Indigenous wisdom, scientific knowledge, and the teachings of plants.* Milkweed Editions.

Learning for Justice. (n.d.). *Let's talk! Discussing race, racism, and other difficult topics with students.* https://www.learningforjustice.org/sites/default/files/general/TT%20Difficult%20Conversations%20web.pdf

Lee, M. J. (2017). *Pachinko.* Grand Central Publishing.

Loewen, J. W. (2007). *Lies my teacher told me: Everything your American history textbook got wrong.* The New Press.

Nguyen, V. T. (2016). *The sympathizer: A novel.* Grove Press.

Orange, T. (2018). *There there.* Vintage Books.

Reynolds, J., & Kiely, B. (2017). *All American boys.* Caitlyn Dlouhy Books.

Ryan, C. L., Patraw, J. M., & Bednar, M. (2013). Discussing princess boys and pregnant men: Teaching about gender diversity and transgender experiences within an elementary school curriculum. *Journal of LGBT Youth, 10*(1–2), 83–105.

Sáenz, B. A. (2014). *Aristotle and Dante discover the secrets of the universe.* Simon & Schuster Books for Young Readers.

Sanchez, A. (2003). *Rainbow boys.* Simon & Schuster Books for Young Readers.

Santiago, E. (2006). *When I was Puerto Rican: A memoir.* Da Capo Press.

Senzai, N. H. (2010). *Shooting Kabul.* Simon & Schuster.

Thomas, A. (2017). *The hate u give.* Balzer & Bray.

Whitehead, C. (2016). *The Underground Railroad.* Knopf Doubleday.

Whitehead, C. (2020). *The Nickel boys.* Knopf Doubleday.

Woodson, J. (2019). *Red at the bone.* Riverhead Books.

Zinn, H. (2015). *A people's history of the United States: 1492–present.* Harper Perennial Modern Classics.